Coraggio!

Lessons for Living From an Italian Grandmother
The Courage to Believe in Miracles

By
Lisa K. Gigliotti, J.D.

Dedication

To beautiful Aunt Mary Marchio,

Who taught me to always, *always* believe in healing miracles.

Who after a tragic accident left me motherless and in a
wheelchair at age twenty-five, never failed to send a
"Love, Aunt Mary" card on my birthday.

And who at age 62 achieved a college degree in hospice care
so she could embolden the faith of those dying of cancer,
yet paradoxically taught us about the power of faith as she spent
the next ten years in a courageous battle with her
own relentless cancer.

With heartfelt appreciation
To Mary George whose talented, beautiful imagery breathed
spirit into *Coraggio!*

With profound gratitude
To Ruth Brown Sanborn, for a life-time of spiritual ponderings,
and whose theological learnedness and deep love of God
were invaluable in editing *Coraggio!* –Courage to
Believe in Miracles.

Table of Contents

Coraggio! Courage to Believe in Miracles

Prologue

Coraggio! Lessons for Living from an Italian Grandmother
The Courage to Believe in Miracles

At the age of twenty, I could not imagine my life's vocation being anything other than a surgeon. I was robust; running one to three miles each day under the ever-changing colors of the magnificent trees in East Grand Rapids, Michigan. Halfway through my pre-medical studies, I was unstoppable in my quest to become a medical missionary. God had given me the intellect and a body of sheer force; I would return the favor to God by healing the souls and bodies of His broken people.

At my father's home for summer break, I was awakened in the middle of the night by my own screams of agonizing pain, my athlete's body locked into a pain-tightened ball.

One week after having blood drawn, I returned to the family doctor to hear him matter-of-factly proclaim I would be crippled by rheumatoid arthritis, I would never go to medical school and I would spend the rest of my life in an institution.

I drove straight to Nonna's house with the negative

prognostication I had just received. Nonna (Italian for grandmother) was the matriarch of our Italian-American family. I conveyed that the doctor predicted I would eventually be crippled. There was no wailing by Nonna. There was no assurance from Nonna that someone would take responsibility for me. There was no expression of feeling sorry. That was not the *Calabrese testadura* (stubborn Southern Italian) way. After the silence of a lengthy pause, Nonna softly urged:

"*Coraggio, Leeza. Coraggio.*" ("Courage, Lisa. Courage.")

It took me years to fully understand the power of *Coraggio* and the impactful power behind Nonna's three simple words.

Within weeks of the diagnosis, I moved to California where my mother and her mother, *Nagymama* (Hungarian for grandmother) lived. California's year-round climate was more arthritis-friendly than Michigan and its harsh winters. Despite a damning decree from the doctor, I finished my pre-medical studies at Mount Saint Mary's College, the bucolic campus overlooking the Pacific Ocean from a Santa Monica mountain top.

My pre-med graduation victory had been short-lived. In the three years since diagnosis, the ferocity of rheumatoid arthritis had eaten most of my joint linings. The cartilage **between** my knees completely gnawed raw to the underlying bone, I lived the next two years from a wheelchair or in bed locked painfully into a curled ball. I was fortunate in that I had moved into my mother's and Nagymama's Woodland Hills, California apartment. Out of necessity, our shared admiration of music and God, and the bonds of maternal love, we three were inseparable. From the small apartment these two women lovingly and devotedly fed, bathed, and toileted their adult daughter and granddaughter, with dogged determination that their efforts would restore my ability to walk again. Even more, with unmatched determination, these women stormed the heavens with fervent, openhearted, **English, Hungarian, and Latin worded** prayers that I would be miraculously healed.

At the age of twenty five, I could never have imagined that life could inflict more than one tragedy on me, much less imagine that two additional misfortunes of even greater and more sinister character would unfold in the near future.

The two years of care and prayers tendered by my mother and grandmother had reaped in me strength sufficient to be out of bed for longer periods of time during the day, and for me to propel myself within the apartment using my heels to move the manual wheelchair. Christmas 1986 was upon us and, with it, plans for an out-of-state holiday road trip. As more items were packed in the small hatchback car it became apparent my wheelchair would not fit. There was also the problem of how I would navigate bathroom and meal stops. In a time before the *Americans with Disabilities Act*, there would be obstacles preventing me from accessing these facilities in the wheelchair; not to mention it would be necessary to unload and reload the heavy wheelchair from an already overstuffed car at every stop. It was easy for me to announce I was okay with forgoing the trip; we would celebrate Christmas upon Mom's and Nagymama's return. It never occurred as they drove away without me that day before Christmas Eve, the ones most precious to me in all the world would never return alive.

The days following the accident that took my mother's life and left Nagymama in critical condition, were crammed with emotional and physical stress. My mother's and Nagymama's enticing auras of regality and vivacity had endeared them to hundreds of friends world-wide. Literally hours were spent delivering news of the tragedy to the friends by phone. Calls to family members in Hungary and across Europe had to be made during hours when I should have been sleeping. But I did not care; I was afraid to sleep. Falling into exhausted dreams, I would desperately search and sobbingly find my mother. With broad smile she would reassure, "Here I am Lisa. See? I am okay. There was a mistake...I didn't die..." Or I would hear **in my mind** my Nagymama's heavily Hungarian accented voice tenderly call my name. In both instances I woke to find a tear-soaked pillow and a gut wrenched by reality.

The emotional and physical stress escalated. There were insurance company matters to be sorted out with Nagymama's out-of-state emergency room and intensive care unit bills. There were inquiries from the out-of-state coroner to be responded to, always laced with disturbing facts about the moments leading up to, and the cause of, Mom's death. It all had to be dealt with. At the small kitchen table in the small apartment, I sat in the manual wheelchair making and receiving calls on a telephone whose long wall-attached cord was my only connection with the world. There were three generations of women's belongings in an apartment I could no longer afford. Stress! I numbly plodded through the aftermath of an unfathomable tragedy… ever-mounting, emotional and physical stress.

A couple days after Christmas, someone pushed my wheelchair to the front of Mount Saint Mary's Chapel so I could present my mother's eulogy. I began speaking in a strong voice, determined to memorialize the beauty of my mother's soul and joyful countenance without tarnishing it with a cracking or crying voice. After several sentences, my voice sounded nasally, similar to that of a munchkin from the *Wizard of Oz* movie. Quickly the nasally voice disintegrated into a garble, as though I had consumed a sizeable gulp of whiskey punch from the Land of Oz.

Watching the 1987 New Year's Day Rose Bowl game a few days later, my vision doubled and I saw two football players on the field where only one had appeared a moment before. In the weeks that followed, my arms felt as if they were 100 pound lead weights.

I hid the symptoms from others as best I could. How could they believe another tragedy—the third within as many years—could happen to me? Surely, I was turning into a paranoid hypochondriac.

When my facial muscles became too weak to chew or

swallow and I began having problems taking a deep breath, I called my rheumatologist. I explained to her I had symptoms similar to, as I learned during my pre-medical studies, a lesser-known neuromuscular disease. In fact, I had seen a photo of Aristotle Onassis with his eyelids taped to his forehead shortly before he died from this rare neuromuscular disease. Less than a week after the blood tests were drawn, the rheumatologist called me back to tell me I was correct: I had myasthenia gravis.

With rheumatoid arthritis, my body made antibodies that attacked my joints. With myasthenia gravis, my body was again making errant antibodies; this time that blocked the receptors on my muscles, rendering certain muscles unable to move. The result was fatigued arm, leg, face, neck, and eye muscles. When one or more muscles controlling my eyes became fatigued, they could no longer hold their position; this caused me to see double of one object. When the muscles of my face and necked pooped out, I could not swallow and liquids would dribble out of limp lips, or I would choke without the ability to cough free the trapped item. It was the fatigue of my respiratory muscles that caused the greatest imminent threat to my life.

The onset of myasthenia gravis was relentless and stubbornly unresponsive to massive doses of daily steroids and a drug that acted like snake anti-venom. I was hospitalized with the possibility that I would be placed on a respirator whereby oxygen pressure would force my lungs to expand. The respirator would help me breathe, giving my weakened respiratory muscles an opportunity to recuperate. Being hospitalized also made it convenient for me to receive plasma pheresis treatments, a more aggressive attempt to stabilize what was an exacerbated medical condition. Plasma pheresis, a type of blood dialysis, would filter out antibodies from my blood in an attempt to lessen the number of defective antibodies impeding my muscles from working.

The plasma pheresis brought me out of the acute myasthenic crisis, but my medical condition continued to be unstable. I was ready for discharge from the hospital but the doctors ordered several additional weeks of outpatient plasma pheresis. I had no car; I had not even taken one step in the prior two years. My entire local family had been killed in an accident. It was the convergence of several unthinkable circumstances that landed me in a nursing home close to the hospital. A medical transportation van transported me to and from the hospital for pheresis, and nurse aides fed, bathed, and helped me to the toilet me after each exhausting day-long blood pheresis.

I was not helping God's broken people; it was I who was totally dependent on others to help me. I wasn't with my classmates in medical school. My friends had their new homes with their new husbands and new babies; I had a new home, but with housemates whose conversation was stunted by dementia. My wide-eyed roommate was in a persistent vegetative state. With no phone in my room in a time when cell phones were non-existent; I had no means of communicating with the outside world. Each time the nurse aides scurried out of the room with my call button out of reach, they took away my voice. When the nursing home staff folded my wheelchair and moved it against the wall on the opposite side of the room, they took away my legs.

Worse yet was when the lights were dimmed and the door shut at night, and the cries of dementia from other residents diminished. In the stillness and darkness of that nursing home room, the tormentors would start. Scenes from my mother's and Nagymama's car accident played across my mind. I had read the police report and coroner's report. I knew what happened to my mother's body; the medical description of every trauma that caused her death. In my emotionally exhausted state I battled to force away these painful thoughts, only to lose to a vividly detailed rerun. When the reruns started to play in my mind, I attempted to force a redo of the events leading to my mother's departure. I hoped that if I could visualize Mom and me in a loving embrace, if I could see myself telling her "I Love You!", it would replace the reality that I had withheld my love for her in her last living moments.

My silent cry to the heavens: *God, help me! I am slipping down a dark, slimy vortex with no foothold!*

In my soul's most desperate moment, in the dark stillness of night in that nursing home room, I heard a familiar voice, Nonna's voice, softly urging,

"*Coraggio, Leeza. Coraggio.*"

AND I GOT IT! I understood the power of *Coraggio*.

I thought back on Nonna's Old World stories... they were laced with adversity. Often Nonna preceded the Old World stories with:

> "Now *Cumari Teresa*...you remember *Cumari Teresa*? She's the one...you know...eight of her eleven children lived? Well, *Cumari Teresa* when she was first married..."

And off went Nonna telling a tale involving *Cumari Teresa* that had nothing to do with childbirth.

Another example...

> "You remember *Zia Carmella*? She's the one whose grandson was swept away by a big wave, his little body returned by the sea but with no life left? Yes, that *Zia Carmella*..."

Nonna proceeded to tell a story involving Zia Carmella where the dead grandson was never mentioned.

Cumari Teresa? I knew she rose from the childbirth bed, whether her baby had lived or not, and started the pasta pot boiling because no matter how weak she felt, the need to feed her family trumped her feelings of personal pain or fatigue.

Zia Carmella? I knew despite heavy grief at the loss of a young grandson, on Tuesday mornings she marched with an equally heavy bundle of flour to the sole brick oven shared by the townsfolk. The weekly oven use time allotted for Aunt Carmella's family was Tuesday morning and if her family was to have those round, flat Calabrese loaves of bread that week, she had to claim her designated oven time, whether or not she emotionally felt up to baking in public.

I recognized that to these Old World figures hardship was a part of life. Better said, hardship was a part of *living* life. There would be drought, wars, and untimely deaths. Troubled times were assured, yet the figures in Nonna's stories did not shrink from a robust life in an attempt to avoid the risk of misfortune. Nor did they secret themselves away after tragedy. They accepted their lot in life and *made no excuses* to avoid work, relationships, love, and celebration.

Thus, at twenty five years old I came to know—in the desperate dark stillness of night in that nursing home—I had everything within I would need to survive… and to live a fulfilled life with joy and purpose… and it started with having courage.

Sheer courage propelled me through law school and careers as a disability advocate, policy advisor to the Michigan Senate, to a governor, and now as an administrative law judge. Along the way, courage got me through thoracic surgery to remove my thymus, four knee replacement surgeries, two ankle fusion surgeries, and two **elbow** replacement surgeries.

In Nonna's *Lezione Uno* (Lesson One) of *Coraggio! Lessons For Living From An Italian Grandmother Despite Illness, Pain, & Loss* (Gigliotti, 2009), we learned about how Nonna discovered the importance of courage. In Nonna's *Lezione Due* (Lesson Two), we learned about how, with the courage to take charge of health (to identify aspects of our health we have control over and act to bring wellness to those aspects), we can live a fulfilled life of purpose and joy despite illness. In Nonna's *Lezione Tre* (Lesson Three), we learned that with courage to take charge of attitude (the "Oh Happy Day" game to foster an attitude of gratitude; the no-blame and reframe techniques to propel us forward), we can live a fulfilled life of purpose and joy despite pain and loss. From Nonna's *Lezioni Uno, Due, e Tre* we learned to chuck aside the "I can't because…" excuses and take the "With courage I can…" pledge.

Embedded in Nonna's stories was a formidable

characteristic in each Old World figure…that of an internal life centered on God. Not a theologian or even an assigned priest among them, each day for these people was lived in constant inner dialogue with the Divine. The stories portrayed simple townsfolk rich in their expressions of thanksgiving to the Divine, unceasingly, throughout each day. They unapologetically implored God and His agents in times of desperation. In these times of supplication and praise, my Italian ancestors had an undaunted sense that God was on their side, and that God and His agents would pull them through any calamity.

How was it that the God known by my Italian ancestors was a kind companion and rescuer, yet the God I knew was vengeful, punishing me with two severe and restricting diseases, and robbing me of my two beloved maternal caregivers? In this book, journey with me as I learn *Nonna's Lezione Quattro*: the courage to believe in miracles. *Buon Viaggio!* (A Good Voyage to you!)

CHAPTER 1

"O Madon′!"

(Oh Blessed Virgin Mary!)

The courage to experience a benevolent and loving God.
The courage to believe in hope, prayer and miracles when
faced with the impossible.
The courage to believe beloved departed are enveloped in
love that surpasses all understanding.

NONNA TOLD ME THE BLESSED VIRGIN MARY STORY MANY TIMES
throughout my life. At each telling she would lower her
voice in grave seriousness…
 speak slowly…
  with transfixed gaze…
   as if she had witnessed the miracle
   herself.
The miracle had, in actuality, been witnessed by her

mother. Young in age, her mother Giuseppina had been crouched on the stone-paved street in front of her church, enraptured in gleeful play with two *ragazze* (little girls). The church in Pedivigliano, Italy, *Chiesa SS. Pietro e Paolo,* (Saints Peter and Paul Church) as with many of the small towns in Provencio Coscenza, was the cornerstone of the community.

Chiesa SS. Pietro e Paolo's grey craggy, stacked-stone structure was a contrast to Pedivigliano's smooth apricot stucco buildings, as if to signify its role as guardian of the *paese* (town). Six grey, shallow flat stone steps rose to massively heavy, arched, wood plank doors. The façade above the doors was unremarkable but for a plain rectangular window near the red, clay tile roof. Throughout *Pedivigliano's* history, four of the town's strongest men processed out from the arched doorway and down those stone steps, struggling to carry the platform bearing a five foot tall plaster statue of the Blessed Virgin Mary cuddling a Baby Jesus in her arms. Both *la Madonna e il Bambino* (Blessed Virgin Mary with Baby Jesus) were reverently adorned with gold metallic-crowns. Each year, the men and their weighty, sacred cargo led a procession through narrow streets on the day designated for all the townsfolk to venerate *la Madonna e il Bambino.*

On the day of the miracle my great-grandmother Giuseppina crouched between the other girls, partly facing the church façade. Cotton dresses covered the bare legs and feet of the girls as they sat on the stones and dirt, facing each other. Giuseppina's thick mop of black shiny coils bounced against her olive-tanned cheeks as she giggled and threw back her head in enjoyment of the child's play.

As the story was told, by divine prompting or in throws of giggles, Giuseppina glanced up from the childhood game toward the apex of the *Chiesa.* Her eyes caught a flash of pastel color and sheen luminosity. *O…La Madonna? (Oh… the Blessed Virgin Mary?) Could it be?* She gasped without breaking her gaze. Yes. Yes!! It was her…the Blessed Virgin Mary…in a momentary perch at the window near the top of the church. Giuseppina's black eyes rounded and widened at the sight. Mesmerized, she witnessed Blessed Virgin Mary take flight… slowly alighting from the window sill…

into the bright blue Southern Calabria sky. An indescribably resplendent Immaculate Mary was escorted; a gloriously majestic angel with large feathery wings and flowing robes accompanied her at each side, slightly below her reverently elevated position.

"*La Madonna! La Madonna!*" Giuseppina shouted in astonishment!

Her lighted face turned upward, eyes following the celestial beings' ascent toward the heavens. Alarmed, her small friends followed the gaze of Giuseppina's gaping eyes in time to witness the three holy figures soar to lofty heights. They stared until their human eyes could no longer detect the forms enveloped in distant heavens. Giuseppina made the Sign of the Cross and kissed the hand that touched her forehead, heart, left and right shoulders to form the Roman Catholic symbol. The friends quickly followed her reverent gesture. Although her companions were youthful, with their witness of the event, Giuseppina's miracle was corroborated. *Un miracolo per Giuseppina!* (A miracle for Josephine!) This blessed apparition of divine grace was treated throughout Giuseppina's life as if she had been crowned with a bejeweled tiara in recognition of God's favor.

Because her mother had been chosen to witness a sacred apparition, Nonna had reasoned that she, too, had been chosen to receive God's special favor. She knew God as a benevolent God. She was not the unforgivable sinner, punished by God for her impure actions and castigated for the fallen actions of the tempted Biblical Eve, as taught by the Catholic doctrine of her day. To the contrary, Nonna's benevolent God protected her at all times. Nonna's God loved her without vengeful judgment or reproach. Nonna's relationship with God was not the result of an intellectual theological debate. The relationship was pure in its simplicity: she simply accepted God's love and felt God's protection. And it was from reliance on God's unconditional love and protection that she drew the courage to step assuredly and boldly into the difficult and unpleasant challenges that awaited her in life.

Because of her mother's apparition miracle her mother

experienced, Nonna developed a lifelong Marian devotion. Each spring she directed my brothers and father, straining and grunting under the heavy plaster weight, to carry the three-foot tall Virgin Mary statue from the lowly winter garage shelter to the tree stump in the garden where it would be venerated. The light blue, pink and white painted statue was strategically placed so Nonna could see it from the kitchen window. *Perfetto* (perfect). Nonna would gaze upon the consoling figure of Our Lady from the kitchen, where she spent immeasurable hours preparing meals for her family. During winter months when the statue was safely stored from the harsh elements, she lovingly repainted the figure's delicate and solemn features. Another sign of Nonna's devotion to the Virgin Mary was her rosary. This rosary, five decades of light blue beads resembling miniature robin eggs, was always within reach on her bedside dresser. Then there was the aged, yellowed replica of the *Mater Dolorosa* (Mother of Sorrows) which hung on the wall opposite Nonna's bed. The black and white print displayed expressions of prayerful reflection, meditation and melancholy. As long as I can remember, this was the image that Nonna gazed upon each night before falling asleep, and that greeted her each morning as she awoke.

In times of disbelief, disgust or slight distress, Nonna would stare straight ahead, hands tightly gripping the armrest of her rust-colored, velveteen reclining chair, and mumble to herself, "*Mama Mia! Mama Mia! Mama Mia!*" These utterances were followed by three clicking sounds produced by the application of her tongue to her palate, as she simultaneously shook her head back and forth. From her reclining chair in the living room, she was surrounded by images of her beloved divine intercessors. For guidance and intercession, Nonna looked to the gargantuan two feet by three feet poster of *Il Papa* (Pope John Paul II). She had the poster framed after she attended Mass presided over by the revered pope at the Pontiac Silverdome on his 1987 visit to Detroit. *Il Papa* hung assuredly facing her on the west living room wall. On the wall above her recliner was a framed photo of Father Solanus Casey, a Capuchin friar known for intercessory miracles. Father Solanus' presence over her was for protection and intercession. These framed sentries protected her and interceded on her behalf when she needed divine assistance. They provided her with a daily feeling of security.

But when Nonna was in extreme distress, she would plaintively cry out,

"O Madon'!" ("Oh, Blessed Mary!")

In emergency rooms and hospital rooms, as sympathetic medical professionals worked to extract blood or perform some other medical intrusion on her petite, frail 90 year-old body, the cry *"O Madon'!"* could be heard down the hall and in adjacent rooms. At first I was concerned that the cry would disturb the other patients. I would try to comfort and reassure Nonna, hoping that it would also quiet her. As she battled against end stage congestive heart failure that necessitated many hospital visits and procedures, and which would inevitably take her life, I finally understood Nonna's *"O Madon'!"* as her cry for Divine intervention. After all, she was heir to a special dispensation from God and, as such, she could call on Him via the Blessed Virgin Mary to directly assist her in her time of need. From that time forward, I never tried to quiet her piercing, desperate pleas to the Madonna. Instead, I would stroke her cheek and gently sweep her hair back from her pain-sweated brow while whispering reassurances in her ear. Silently, I, too, was calling on the Madonna. There were times when Nonna's physical agony and excruciating pain were more than I could bear to witness silently, that *I* pleaded out loud for mercy:

> *"O Madonna, as mother of us both…oh great-grandma Giuseppina as mother of Nonna…oh Aunt Connie as daughter of Nonna…please any other heavenly being; please, please, **PLEASE** bring this sweet, suffering woman peaceful relief!"*

For many people, unwavering faith persists even (and especially) through experiences of tragedy of body and spirit. For these people, they abide in an abundance of peace, fortitude, and hope from the spiritual consolation they know in every aspect of their daily lives. For others, seemingly insurmountable physical challenge or crushing grief leaves them with feelings of spiritual desolation, the river of peace, fortitude, and hope parched and dried, their cries, *Oh God, why have you abandoned me?* unanswered. For which scenario does courage play a role?

For both.

Courage is the underlying bedrock of spiritual consolation and spiritual desolation. It takes courage to stand firm in faith...to maintain hope...to continue to believe in miracles...despite insurmountable challenge, unrelenting pain, and devastating loss. Fierce, determined courage is necessary in order to believe in any kind of higher, benevolent power when cries for mercy appear to go unanswered, and the soothing well of comfort seems never more to spring forth reassurance.

I have had a strong spiritual sense for as long as I can remember. Yet it took more than a decade after my initial rheumatoid arthritis diagnosis before I developed a sense of God as a soothing, loving, protector, and not a God of punishment. Instead of a judgmental God who inflicts penalties, I came to know God as the warming healer of my soul. Witnessing Nonna's courageous faith – her simple belief in a benevolent and sheltering God – illumined me and led to my experiential conversion. It was Nonna's courage and belief in Omnipresent benevolence that gave me en*courage*ment during my most desperate times.

May you possess the courage to:
- Believe that a benevolent higher power surrounds you.
- Sense the soothing, loving, healing protection of God.
- Know that during periods of isolation and desperation, soothing spiritual consolation will come again.

CHAPTER 2

Punishment

RELIGION. GOD. MIRACULOUS OCCURRENCES. THESE SUBJECTS ARE often taboo in many circles. Public discourse about God and religion are stifled or withheld for fear of impropriety or criticism. I discuss them openly because for many, myself included, they are the critically essential realities of life. The phenomena of spiritual-based healings and miracle healings are extensively written about and widely documented.

This is your punishment from God. This was my first spiritual thought, connecting religion to my initial diagnosis, overwhelming joint pain, and loss of physical abilities from rheumatoid arthritis. During high school I looked older than most of my friends, and was the natural born leader of the group. I violated Michigan law and purchased alcohol for my friends and myself even though I was a minor. I also kissed boys. Although modest in event, there had been several kissed boys through high school and the first year of college. The first few years after diagnosis, the assault on my body from rheumatoid arthritis was brutal. In the long, lonely hours of screaming pain, I was convinced that consuming alcohol and kissing boys, even though refraining from any further sins of the flesh, was a cause of my rheumatoid arthritis. I was being punished. Worst of the offenses was the fact that I took God's name in vain, sometimes with a swear word attached. Was that not the most flagrant violation of one of the Ten Commandments? *Yes!* Were there not a mere Ten requests that God asked me to obey…yet I failed to meet even these few wishes? Yes! To disrespect God in such a foul manner was the sure clincher. Yes, *rheumatoid arthritis is your punishment.* Thus my initial spiritual response to the virulent affliction was to assume it was direct retribution for my disobedience and sin. *Accept the punishment. Then offer up your pain and suffering in thanksgiving for the pain and suffering Jesus endured for you and for other sinners.*

Within a couple of years, the way in which I reflected spiritually on my physical affliction evolved from that of direct punishment to a more utilitarian approach: *Perhaps the suffering and loss I was experiencing could be **useful**.*

During my junior and senior years of undergraduate study, I lived in the dormitory adjacent to the campus chapel. Each weekday morning at 7:30, the Sisters of Saint Joseph of Carondelet gathered for Mass in the Mount St. Mary's Chapel. Some mornings, I attended morning Mass with those beautiful servants of God. The front pews occupied by the Sisters, I respectfully sat several heavily varnished pews behind, watching as they gracefully filed into place and knelt in reflective preparation for the Eucharist.

In the 1980s, several Sisters continued to don the traditional habit of the Congregation of the Sisters of Saint Joseph of Carondelet. The habit was elaborate and beautiful. Across the shoulders of the ankle-length, gathered black dress hung the *guimpe*, a twelve-inch, rounded and starched white bib. An equally starched white crown, (called a *wimple*) framed the Sister's face, over which a long black veil draped down her back. Only the face and hands of these holy, reverent women were uncovered. A large crucifix hung around the Sister's neck and dangled below the *guimpe*, a stark contrast against the large, white bib. A large rosary was clipped to the right side of her habit at the waist. However, given that it was the post-Vatican II 1980s, most of the Sisters wore secular, albeit modest, garb. I admired the Sisters' devotion to their faith and their mission to educate young women. I was especially and deeply appreciative of their kindness toward me.

With the Sisters in place for Mass, it was time for me to kneel in prayerful preparation for the Eucharist…or to come as close to kneeling as my arthritic body would allow. I scooted forward in the pew and leaned forward, braced by my forearms against the back of the pew in front of me, ignoring the ache within my inflamed elbows. I could no longer kneel on my arthritis-ravaged knees, but felt this was a good effort. I meditated on the Mass, deeply engrossed in the purpose and intent of each part of the liturgy, *the work of the people.* Against the north wall of the praedella on which the altar rested, the chapel's heavy blood-red curtains draped and contrasted with the white marble steps that led to the altar.

> *Dear Lord, please forgive all my sins. Cleanse my soul so that I may be ready to receive your precious Body and Blood. Help me to rise above the pain of rheumatoid arthritis, so that this day I may learn what I need and that I may be your love and your joy to all I meet…*

Mount St. Mary's College campus was perched atop one of the Santa Monica Mountains. A retired priest from somewhere "off the Mount" faithfully appeared every morning to celebrate the Mass.

"Father looks about eighty years old, don't ya think?"
I whispered the inquiry during the Liturgy of the Word to my Italian-American biology classmate Maria, who sometimes sat next to me at morning Mass.

"No way. My guess is…Father is closer to ninety years old," she replied.
But there he was, bless his dedicated heart, every morning, presiding on the altar, arms outstretched as he uttered the long passages of the Eucharistic prayer. His voice would begin to fade, words became mumbled and his head would drop forward. Silence. His arms remained outstretched but

there was no detectable movement. Continued silence. No one made a sound.

As quietly as possible I whispered: "Maria. Do you think...perhaps Father has fallen asleep?"

Well...I wasn't meaning to be irreverent...but maybe he had fallen asleep. After all he was pretty old, it was much too early in the morning, and he had certainly risen even earlier to drive up the mountain to campus. Maria tilted her head toward mine to assure none of the Sisters would hear:

"Maybe...he died? Right here...in the middle of Mass. Do you think someone should check?"

But after thirty seconds or so, Father's head would bob back up and he would return to reciting from the Sacramentary... as if no pause had occurred.

After Mass, the Sisters would file out of the pews and chapel, appearing to silently contemplate the Mass or the upcoming day, sometimes nodding a wordless greeting to others... and to me. One morning, I had lingered in the pew to bother God with a few more of my petitions. A professor nun that several of my friends had as an instructor also was delayed after Mass. Although I had had only a few brief prior conversations with her, she greeted me in the aisle as we were simultaneously exiting. There were only a few women present in the chapel. Sister asked me how I was doing emotionally with the pain of my unrelenting arthritis. I started my response by remarking about identifying with Jesus' suffering. I was curtly interrupted with:
"and don't give me that Jesus suffering on the cross so I will too and offer it up to Him crap!"
I was surprised, to say the least. *I did not know that nuns were allowed to say the word "crap."*

Second, I thought a woman devoted to religious life, in fact *married* to Jesus, as was understood with vows taken by nuns, would understand my reflection better than anyone else. Why, I had been raised in a faith whose focus was on a man torturously hanged from a cross, pierced and bloodied, with an expression of mortal woundedness and death. I was taught that I had been redeemed by His pain and suffering, and the very least I could offer in return was to bear my pain and suffering humbly while offering it up to Him. I had sworn blind belief in the Mysterious changing of wine into His precious blood. I had drunk this blood at least once a week.

Mom told me I was supposed to offer up my pain for the sins of others.

There were multitudes of saints who had borne persecution and bodily pain as penance for themselves and for the indiscretions of all sinners. When I was crabby and demanding, my mother would inquire, "Why can't you be more like the saints?" I would freeze with guilt at the inquiry. "Remember Saint Bernadette. After seeing visions of the Blessed Virgin Mary in Lourdes, she entered a convent. Saint Bernadette suffered from a prolonged and painful illness. Her Mother Superior ordered her to scrub the floors on her hands and knees…and she did so without complaint… even though ill and in excruciating pain" was my mother's rhetorical admonition to me.

Ouch!

The chastisement of failure to endure my own physical trials in a holy manner stung bitterly. After this type of reproach, I really did try to emulate the examples of the saints. It followed that I tried to become as saintly in my daily life as was humanly possible, a spiritually treacherous and psychologically dangerous path. But in the evolution of my faith, as I tried to derive meaning out of a life-altering chronic illness, becoming a saint could be more purposeful than a mere utilitarian view of being punished.

It is human nature to attempt to find logical explanations for unfair occurrences. After my first set of knee replacements enabled me to walk again, I engaged in coursework to become a hospital chaplain. The chaplaincy training was conducted at the University of Michigan Mott Children's Hospital. I thought I could use my own experiences with disease and death to give hope and reassurance to others.

This is the perfect opportunity. At least you will be working in a hospital until you are strong enough to pursue your life goal and passion: a medical degree and practice.

Of all the years of education, I found the chaplaincy course hospital practicum was by far the most difficult. Parents would blame themselves for their child's serious illness or birth defect.

"God is punishing me. What else could it be? My newborn is absolutely innocent."

Or parents would be openly hostile toward God.

"I don't believe there is a God...how could anyone let my young child suffer like this?"

> *How are you going to respond to the parent? Why are you at a loss? Think of something...Please Lord...let me know what I should say. Should I say anything at all?*

I was the chaplain student, but I did not know what to say. Any thought that entered my brain sounded like a cardboard cliché to me. I knew, of course, that retribution for what the parent had done, or did not do, was not the reason for their child's suffering. Silence ensued. Awkward, prolonged, silence. I did not know how to respond and did not offer any theological explanation or flowery encouragement; I did not have even a single word of consolation. I had to be honest with myself: I did not know why some people endured horrible diseases or died in senseless auto accidents. Needless to say, I never became a hospital chaplain. It was not until many years later through Nonna's example, that I recognized God is benevolent...not punishing. At the slam of rheumatoid arthritis against a twenty year old body, I had not had sufficient time to emotionally or spiritually process all the facets of the Benevolent One's true meaning. At first it took a lot of deprogramming before I could rebuild on the love and compassion theme. My belief that God is a kind, loving and caring being only came after slogging through the muck-field of the many Italian-Catholic heavies I had absorbed and integrated from my childhood.

May you possess the courage to:
- Believe that God is one who does not punish, but rather bestows love and protection upon you and your loved ones.

CHAPTER 3

Guilt

GUILT. THE ITALIAN CATHOLIC UPBRINGING IS LADEN WITH THE HEAVY, tormenting yoke of guilt. Oh, and in my family we played the guilt game well. Guilt burdened my every decision, my every action, my every word. Guilt stifled me to inaction and even to silence. Round and round went the saddling yoke of guilt; plodding the asses' grist mill.

For those who have not experienced day-to-day life from a wheelchair, let me point out that eye level of a person in a wheelchair is equivalent to the level of a zipper on a pair of pants. Most people who walk upright do not crouch down or sit next to a person sitting in a wheelchair. The result? People who walk upright talk down to the person sitting in the wheelchair. At least this was my experience when I was confined to a wheelchair. When my arthritic neck grew sore and tired from craning upward, or when there was a lull in the conversation, my head would automatically return to a looking-straight-forward position. This meant that the zipper on the pants of the person I was speaking to was right there in front of me, in my direct line of vision! When I realized this, I became embarrassingly mortified and quickly looked away.

This was the situation I found myself in one day when a college friend and her brother chatted with me, they standing and I seated in a wheelchair. My friend's brother was my younger sister's age. He was very handsome, suavely charming, and interested in dating my gorgeous sister! The conversation proceeded in a polite enough manner when the brother suddenly stepped directly in front of me and, looking down toward me, asked,

"Do you believe that Jesus Christ is your Lord and Savior?"

I did not identify myself as a "born-again Christian." Rather, I considered myself a "born-with Christian," experiencing Jesus as a messenger of love and peace. This is what I heard in the Scripture readings every time I went to Mass. I profoundly felt Jesus' love and peace even before my First Holy Communion at age seven, and thus answered,

"Why yes! Of course!"

No sooner had I given my response, the brother retorted,

"Well, it says in the Bible that Jesus healed those who believed in Him. So you must not truly believe in Him. If you truly believed in Jesus you would be healed by now."

The words were excoriating. His eyes stared burning judgment at me. *Condemnation!* I wanted to break the spell of his glaring stare, but he was standing uncomfortably close to me. To look away at this moment would mean I would have to look directly at his pant zipper! His sister stood at his side, smiling smugly as if her brother had just performed a most wise and benevolent act of piety. I was certainly not smiling, at least not inwardly. I felt judged, denounced and ripped to pieces in every fiber of my being. If only the brother knew how violently damning his comment was. *Guilt!* I felt gut-churning, major guilt.

*Perhaps…just maybe… at some level you are **not** a true believer. Maybe that **is** why you haven't been healed. Maybe that*

is why your disease has become worse…to the point of living from a wheelchair.

Even though intellectually I knew the strength of my relationship with Jesus and that others could not possibly know its sincerity and depth, that young man's scathing words left me struggling with self-doubt about my spirituality. It was difficult enough to battle my own fears that I was not worthy of Jesus' love. But to hear another person give their assessment of my relationship with Jesus, and judge it to be deficient, was devastating.

This was but one example from many. It is astounding the number of times that people, some of them complete strangers, have rendered similar judgments, that my faith is less than Jesus expects otherwise I would have been healed. In these situations I could barely believe what I was hearing: *Does she not stop to think about how harsh and judgmental these words are as they spew forth from her mouth? Can she not see how potentially hurtful and condemning her words are?* Even though I would intellectually tell myself that the conclusory proclamations of these well-intentioned people were judgmental and unsubstantiated, after all I knew the truth of my actual relationship with Jesus, a deep schism of doubt was torn into my heart. *Maybe she is correct. Maybe I do not believe. Maybe my faith is not strong.*

For many years the New Testament stories of Jesus' miracle healings were hurtful. I was not encouraged by their hope-inducing and healing messages. Rather, I had allowed myself to listen to and believe the rebukes of others. I began to believe I had disappointed Jesus. This left me with feelings of guilt. Could there be enough courage, in heaven or on earth, for me to push aside the guilt I felt for disappointing Jesus so that I could once again feel the powerful peace and love He used to confer on me in the past?

May you possess the courage to:
- Replace guilt and condemnation with hope for, and belief in, healing.
- Replace doubt with a pervasive knowing that God seeks a loving relationship with you at all times and in every circumstance, no matter what.

CHAPTER 4

Shame

As a young schoolgirl, it was a special treat to spend the night at my Nagymama's and Nagypapa's (Hungarian grandmother's and grandfather's) house. It was a long car or bus ride down East Jefferson Avenue from my home on the east side of Detroit, through Downtown Detroit, and continuing on West Jefferson Avenue to their home on the west side of Detroit. The path followed Lake St. Clair as it emptied into the Detroit River and was a clash of contrasts; from the biggest, most elegant mansions of Grosse Pointe, to the dilapidated, wood boxes that stood for houses near downtown Detroit.

Nagymama's and Nagypapa's home was a graceful old two-story of solid tan brick. Its huge covered porch welcomed me; wide brick columns rising from the encircling low brick wall.

I never minded the long bus ride with Nagymama or car ride with mother because on arrival I was guaranteed a belly full of delectable Hungarian pastries and a close-up view of the loaded Norfolk Southern trains that rumbled past my grandparents' back fence. To this day I can close my eyes and recall the warmth from Nagymama's ever-producing oven, entrapped by the heavy lead-framed windows. Entrapped also were aromas from the Hungarian delicacies within that oven. Oh! The glorious, heavenly smell of *süt disznóhús* (caraway seed and garlic-encrusted pork roast) and *pogácsa* (dense, crackling and sour cream-based biscuits), dobos torta (multi-layered nut torte) and *Linzer Torte* (red currant jam-filled, lattice-topped pastry).

Also embedded in my "little girl" memories is Sunday Mass at the vast and ornate Holy Cross Hungarian Church. I **loved** going to church with Nagymama. The event meant she would give me one of her white lace, chapel veils to wear on my head. The finishing touch on my Sunday church attire: a pair of her white gloves which, even though stretchy, were too large for my tiny hands... I didn't care. I tightly-grasped within those oversized slippery gloves the rosary and prayer book Nagymama entrusted to me for the sacred event.

We walked several blocks to Holy Cross Hungarian Church. During the walk she kept my white lace chapel veil tucked safely in her purse. I wished I could wear the important white veil all during the walk: past the other Hungarian-American family homes, Agnes Neni's (Great Aunt Agnes') home on the right, then cross the street to the left, past Hortense Neni's (Great Aunt Hortense's) block, and until the splendid steeple cross of the church was visible. As we walked, Nagymama nearly six feet tall with regal posture, and me at her side only half as tall, I gazed up at the homes of Hungarian friends she pointed toward. But when my attention was not directed, I could not help but look down with curiosity at the discolored grey sidewalks and streets. It wasn't until I was much older that I learned Delray, Michigan was adjacent to Zug Island and its industrial inhabitant National Steel Corporation factory. The steel-making factory chugged tons of pollution from its three blast furnaces. So heavy were the contaminated clouds emitted from the perpetually billowing smokestacks, all the sidewalks and buildings were covered in soot; the outside air a fragrance of rotten eggs and dirt.

I figured Nagymama's purpose in withholding my chapel veil deep within the metallic snap-enclosure patent leather purse was to keep safe the white lace from flying off my head and into the staining soot. But after we had climbed the sooty cement steps between the spectacular front spires, pulled back the heavy wooden church doors and stepped inside the darkened foyer, Nagymama shook the crocheted scarf free of folds and placed it on my head. As we walked down the center aisle of the magnificently ornate church with the lace fanciwork adorning my head, I felt I was walking perfectly straight, shoulders back and chin up, for my God. The floor beneath my feet was a pattern of elaborately laid tile, but I dared not look down for fear of my chapel veil slipping from place. I walked proudly next to my beloved Nagymama, my beautifully covered head held high, gloved hands clutching a well-worn leather rosary pouch and Latin prayer book. The intricately carved white altar towered before us. Hand-carved white angels at each side of the altar protected the precious body of Jesus displayed within the royal Monstrance; jagged gold triangular spikes radiating outward like the rays of the sun, as if to symbolize the eminence of the divine love from the consecrated wafer within. The lofty alcove behind the altar was a series of tall, narrow, stained-glass windows; colors rich with the sunlit backlighting it as if the pictures of the saints were made from gemstones. From the Communion rail that cordoned off the sanctuary altar, separating the domain of the priest from the worshipping parishioners, hung white curtains of lace similar to my veil. Nagymama, regal in disposition and fervent in her faith, was befitting of the majestic church.

We halted at Nagymama's preferred pew on the left side of the church in the front third of the expansive church. Before entering the long and rigid wood pew, I performed a respectful curtsy-genuflection to the altar cross and Blessed Sacrament-bearing Tabernacle. I made a deliberate Sign of the Cross with the fingers of my right hand, starting at my forehead, being very careful not to displace the precariously-placed chapel veil. I opened the worn, black leather cover of my prayer book, stared at the Latin and Hungarian words I did not recognize, and pretended to understand what was being said by the priest and recited by the parishioners. It was prior to the Vatican Second Council; the prayers of the Mass being recited entirely in Latin. The priest's Homily delivered to a congregation of Hungarian immigrants, of course, was spoken entirely in the Hungarian language. Spare the word "amen" I did not understand a word the priest or Nagymama said for the following hour. I did not mind. There was plenty of art to explore from where I was sitting. In front of me Nagymama's favorite, the Sacred Heart of Jesus statue set in a small alcove with twinkling votive candles at its feet. On the wall facing me was an enormous painted Biblical scene depicting the Assumption of the Blessed Virgin into heaven. Far, far above me, as if in heaven itself, were elaborate ceiling designs painted in deep pastel tones and bordered in gilded gold. I studied the vaulted ceiling of the alcove above the altar. Every inch was covered in a painted depiction of the Crucifixion of Jesus. The scenes too gruesome for my little girl mind, I immediately diverted my eyes to the painting on the wall to the right of the altar. It was equal in enormity to the painting before me but this Biblical scene was from Luke's gospel, a magnificent Angel Gabriel's annunciation to the Virgin Mary, her head and eyes cast downward in humility.

Every now and then I turned my attention to what was occurring in the Mass. From the time I was born I attended the Mass on Sunday with my family and at least one additional time per week with my classmates once I started Catholic school. Consequently, even though I did not understand the foreign languages, I was able to follow along with the ritual action of the Mass at Holy Cross Catholic Church. Kneeling next to my Nagymama, white-gloved hands pressed palms together and positioned directly below my chin, I was careful to say my prayers, silently and in English, before and after receiving Holy Communion.

Unlike Catholic churches today, the altar was flush against the back wall of the sanctuary. The actions of priest and the congregation members were directed toward the altar and altar cross. This meant the priest, who presided over the Mass from the sanctuary, had his back toward the parishioners, and said prayers in a language many people could not understand. Many Mass-going Catholics felt left out of the ceremony, some felt shame that a priest had to intercede because they were not adequate to speak to God. Thus the role of the churchgoer in the years before the Second Vatican Council became irreverently referred to as "pray, pay, and obey."

With the 1970s changes and reforms that followed the Second Vatican Council, free standing altars were introduced. This one small change in church architecture was incredibly rich in symbol. From the freestanding altar the priest could face the congregation, drawing in churchgoer participation. The Mass became a communal celebration of ritual rich in two millennia of tradition. Gone were the feelings of isolation from God and shame at needing a priest to intercede.

When I was that little girl with beautiful lace headdress, I never knew I should have carried shame for not being good enough to interact with the Lord directly, without a priest interceding on my behalf. Neither did I know that my beautiful lace headdress was symbolic of shame. It was explained to me that women and girls must always cover their heads in church as a symbol of humility and holiness. In actuality, the veiling of women had origins in both Hebrew and Christian scripture. Propriety in worship, as given by St. Paul to the Corinthian people and recorded:

> Be imitators of me, as I am of Christ.
> I praise you because you remember me in everything and hold fast to the traditions, just as I handed them on to you.
> But I want you to know that Christ is the head of every man, and a husband the head of his wife, and God the head of Christ.
> Any man who prays or prophesies with his head covered brings shame upon his head.
> **But any woman who prays or prophesies with her head unveiled brings shame** upon

her head, for it is one and the same thing as if
she had had her head shaved.
For if a woman does not have her head veiled,
she may as well have her hair cut off. ***But if
it is shameful for a woman to have her hair
cut off or her head shaved, then she should
wear a veil.***
A man, on the other hand, should not cover
his head, because he is the image and glory of
God, but woman is the glory of man.
(1 Corinthians 11:1-6 *New American Bible.*)

The prevailing androcentric thought of the first century
was that "*men*" were made in the image of God and as such
were not shamed if they worshipped in front of God with
their heads uncovered. Women, on the other hand, were
thought to be something less than made in God's image.
Therefore, when worshipping God, women veiled their
heads out of shame, especially if they wore hair short. As
the Vatican Second Council occurred at the same time as
the women's liberation movement in the West, one wonders
about the influence of this secular movement on the post-
Council guidelines, which were noticeably absent of the
Hebrew and St. Paul veiling requirement.

In spite of the innocence of my younger childhood, shame
had somehow begun to pervade my religious beliefs and
practices, even long before rheumatoid arthritis attacked my
body. Shame impacted the way I conducted my behavior–or
didn't conduct myself. Shame had a negative effect on how
I viewed myself.

Having my rheumatoid arthritis tied to Biblical themes
of unbelief and a lack of faith was a crushing blow. When
rheumatoid arthritis made it impossible for me to walk,
and had sustained its crippling curse on me for more than
a year, my mother went to the most prominent woman in
her church to ask for her intercessory prayer. My mother
sought prayers that would lead to my healing, or at least
divine revelation as to the cause of my disease. The highly-
revered woman listened to my mother's account of my illness
and hastily pronounced that I was possessed by demons.

For this woman, demonic possession was the obvious cause of my illness. One need only look to the many accounts of disease recorded in the Bible to see this truth. Had not many of the miraculous cures found in Christian scripture come about because Jesus had cast out demons from these sick people? The church lady instructed my mother to warn other members of the church who might come into contact with me of my demonic possession, lest one of my demons possess them. My mother was equally warned against my demons, lest they attempt to seize her.

When my mother returned from the religious consult, I was anxious to hear if there was any hopeful news for a spiritual cure. She avoided eye contact with me, and fumbled for the right words. As careful and measured as her words were, the shame I felt was crushing.

Shortly after my demonic possession was diagnosed, a gentle, elderly church woman came to visit my grandmother. My mother fidgeted nervously, as the woman took great pains to avoid coming too close to me. It was as if they expected a demon to jump off my back and onto her devout shoulder. *Shame!* Shame beyond comprehension. I was horrified at my own repugnance. I felt indelibly unclean. It was difficult enough to like myself from a wheelchair, but to hear others pronounce that I had demons living within me brought with it an incredible and suffocating amount of shame.

Lord, grant me the Courage to know I am cherished.

May you possess the courage to:
- Replace the judgments of others so that you may fully experience the abundant relationship with the Source of Life, the Universe, Divine Energy, God, or whatever you call that which is Life-Giving Force.

Coraggio! Courage to Believe in Miracles

CHAPTER 5

Unworthiness

In 1976, Father Ralph DiOrio was praying over some of his Catholic parishioners when the paralyzed legs of a young boy began to move; the pain in a man with internal bleeding subsided; a woman with mental illness was overcome with peace.

Aunt Mary, wife of my father's first cousin, mailed me the book *A Miracle to Proclaim: Firsthand Experiences of Healing*, published in 1984 by the miracle-performing priest. The book told of twenty-eight people who had received the blessings of miraculous healings from devastating diseases through the Catholic priest's ministry. One day, a frantic, yet excited phone call from Aunt Mary alerted me that Father DiOrio would be traveling to the Cleveland Convention Center on April 27 and 28, 1985, to hold a healing service. Could I attend?

Those who believed this could be my chance for a miracle healing collected money for an airline ticket. Although I was unable to walk, I flew by myself, wheelchair stashed in the cargo hold of the jumbo jet, from Los Angeles to Detroit.

Upon my arrival, my father loaded me and my wheelchair into his car, drove the four hours to Cleveland, and delivered me into the crammed and chaotic Cleveland Convention Center. There were desperate people everywhere! As my father attempted to navigate my manual wheelchair to an open seat, we were surrounded by people with every type of physical and mental disability. Row after row after row of people seated in wheelchairs flowed back from the stage. Although we had arrived early, many others had come even earlier hoping to get close enough to the stage to catch a miracle. People using walkers, canes, and crutches slowly shuffled forward, anxiously seeking a seat as close to the stage as possible. The aisle-ways were jammed. My father spotted one open chair, sat down and spun my wheelchair next to him. *Phew!* It was quite an ordeal, but at least we were sitting next to each other. As I nervously awaited Father DiOrio's arrival, I tried to study the blue text printed on the grey paper service pamphlet we were handed as we entered the convention center. On the first page was a photo of The Most Reverend James Anthony Griffin, the Bishop of Cleveland, followed by a note of personal welcome to the healing service attendees:

Dear Friends in Christ,
April 1985

The Acts of the Apostles speak well of the early Church in which we have our roots. It speaks enthusiastically about the vigor of the early Church; the enthusiasm of the believers of Jesus after His resurrection; the "mighty and powerful deeds" of the Lord that took place through his body of believers.

Endeavoring to have the same kind of enthusiasm, you are gathering together in Easter hope to pray for the sick and the ailing and to join Father Ralph DiOrio in celebrating the healing gifts of the Church.

> In a very special way I want to welcome
> each and every one of you to these services.
> I want to assure you of my support and my
> own personal prayer for healing among God's
> broken ones today.

Oh my. It was quite an impressive endorsement from the highest Catholic official in the Diocese of Cleveland, especially since at that time the Catholic church did not wholeheartedly embrace "speaking in tongues" and "slaying in the spirit," both of which the service pamphlet advised might occur. The Bishop's resounding endorsement of Father DiOrio lent legitimacy to the priest's miraculous healing gifts. My sense of hopeful anticipation grew.

Nonna, Aunt Mary, Aunt Frances, Aunt Josephine, and more of my father's *cugini* (cousins), heck, a full-on Italian-American contingent back home, were praying that Father DiOrio's channeled divine powers would totally heal me so that Dad and I could leave the wheelchair in Ohio and instead run on our own two legs all the way back home! The air was filled with the desperation, the hopes, and the anticipation of hundreds.

Father DiOrio took the stage in white priest collar and full-length white cassock. The long gown flowed behind him as he strode toward center stage revealing his black clunky priest shoes. Silence spread through the convention center as Father DiOrio started speaking and then began to pray. I was praying too. I prayed hard; really, really hard the whole time Father DiOrio was on the stage far in front of me. I felt fervor and tension within myself peak at the same moment. With his eyes closed and his arms outstretched, Father DiOrio announced that the healing of a person in the crowd was occurring at that very moment! *Wait, was it me?* My heart was pounding with anticipation as he continued to describe the healed person. *Hey, was my body starting to feel warm and tingling?* The pamphlet had warned:

> The person (healed) may also experience a
> sensation of extreme heat in the affected area
> or throughout the body, the tingling sensation

or trembling.

Oh no! Father DiOrio's description of the healed person started to clearly identify someone other than me. I felt let down as the air rushed out of my lungs, and my body released its tension. I had not been aware that I had been holding my breath, and had anxiously tensed my body over the possibility that the miracle had to be mine. In retrospect, it was likely the lack of oxygen that led to the tingling sensation I had felt.

At the instant I realized the healing priest was not talking about my healing, I heard a middle-aged woman cry out, her exclamation of joy echoing loudly throughout the cavernous hall. Father DiOrio called for the woman to come forward and claim her miracle. The woman walked to the stage and excitedly exclaimed into a portable microphone that she had come with leg braces and crutches, but no longer needed them. Then another proclamation, another excited cry, another claimed miracle. But there was no miracle for me. I took a quick sideways glance at my father. His eyes were scrunched tight, his mustache twitching as silent, prayerful words fell from his hidden lips. I watched his Adam's apple dip as he swallowed hard. From the day my mother had left him, he had not attended Mass at the Catholic Church on the corner where we used to gather weekly. He and I never really talked about it, but in my teenage wisdom I did not blame him for being angry with God, or resenting religion or whatever it was. But here he was, almost ten years later, praying as hard as he could, fighting back sobs. He strongly believed the healing miracle would occur for me. I strongly believed the healing miracle would occur for me. The praying Italian-American contingent in Michigan believed a healing miracle would occur for me. But it was another person who had just joyously skipped to the stage, exchanging their mobility aid for limbs that had been healed, and that person was not me. Miracle after miracle occurred, but none were mine.

Panic swept over me. What if a miracle did not happen to me? So many people came together to buy me an airline ticket; my dad had driven me all the way to Cleveland, bearing the entire cost; his mother and his cousins were praying for us at this very moment. I did not know to what kind of person God granted healing miracles. Were they a person *deserving* of a miracle? Were they a *good* and *holy* person? What would my dad, grandmother, and other relatives think about me if I came back without the coveted miracle? Would they think that I was not deserving? Would they think that, in actuality, I was not a good person?

No! Wait! The healing event just ended. It could not be over yet. **It…could…not…be…over!** *I had not received a healing miracle!*

Neither my father nor I spoke a word as he steered my wheelchair through long, slow lines of other unhealed people exiting the auditorium with their durable medical equipment. The panic I felt was intermingled with shame. I wondered how many others of the hundreds of infirmed who silently exited with heads hung low, also felt shame that day.

My father and I had a four hour trip home, and with the wheelchair I had hoped to leave in Cleveland in the back of the car. My expectation was that, after my healing miracle, we would cast aside the unnecessary wheelchair, perhaps abandoning it in a corridor of the convention center. But now the old wheelchair occupied a lot of space in the car, even more space than during our journey to Cleveland, as if it was a 100 pound elephant. The rattling of the various metallic parts against itself in its collapsed state seemed to emphasize the awkward silence between my father and me. What would we say to each other in these next interminable hours of highway travel? I knew my father was deeply and innately spiritual. I knew if he spoke, he would say that perhaps the miracle had happened but would not be manifested until tomorrow, or next week. Maybe he would explain that because my rheumatoid arthritis was so severe it would take God several days to regenerate tissue and annihilate inflammation. I supposed that my Dad was disappointed. I wore a heavy mantle of guilt knowing his disappointment was all my fault.

My thoughts turned to Nonna. Who was going to tell

Nonna that the coveted miracle had not been granted? I could see her in my mind, waiting at her front door, a victorious smile on her face visible through the condensation-opaqued storm door window. What words would we use that would inevitably deflate her smile? I know Nonna. She would determinedly freeze that smile onto her face as she peered through the dark to watch my father unload the wheelchair, wheel it to the car door, and lift me into its seat. I had failed. Who would tell Aunt Mary, Aunt Frances, Aunt Josephine, and the rest of the *cugini?* The expectation of being worthy enough to be granted a healing miracle was oppressive. I had sorely failed to meet the expectation. Unworthiness…

Dear Lord, grant me the courage to believe
I am worthy of a healing miracle.

May you possess the courage to:
- Believe your worth.
- Believe you are worthy of healing.
- Believe you are worthy of a miracle.

Chapter 6

Sinner

In my late twenties I attended the religious services of various doctrines in lieu of the Catholic Mass. My spiritual search was precipitated by my desire to nurture a greater self-love and to reduce my ever-present self-doubt and self-criticism. As part of my increasing self-awareness I paid more attention to the self-deprecating words that came from my mouth, and to the events that spurred negative self-thoughts. I also began to believe that "you are what you speak." There is a science to the spoken word; if you think it and then say it, the act of declaration manifests the "it." It is for this reason I avoid saying "I feel sick" or "I am not well." I may have rheumatoid arthritis, I may be in pain, and I may feel exhausted, but to your question, "How are you?" I will answer, "I am well." And you know what? Rheumatoid arthritis, myasthenia gravis and their symptoms aside, I truly am well.

Even though I was working hard during this time to increase my love of self and improve my sense of self-worth,

I found it remarkably difficult, far more difficult than I thought it would be. At the beginning of Catholic Mass, I began to count the number of times I called out loudly that I was a "sinner" or "not worthy" in the prayer responses. I did not want to utter from my own mouth the words that called me a sinner. I did not want to speak of my unworthiness at a liturgical celebration that for decades had been nourishment for my soul. I also wanted to avoid speaking of my unworthiness at a liturgical celebration because it was not true. I did not want to say I was not worthy because I believed I was a child of God, and as such I was worthy of God's love. When I returned to attending Catholic Mass, I refused to say "Lord, I am not worthy" before Communion. My intentional omission of the phrase was not done out of disrespect, ignorance, or belief that I was perfect. It is my constant prayer that my soul be a pure and holy place. This is what I strive for. I did not want the last words I spoke to Christ before I received Him to be, "Come into this unholy and impure place." I could be sincerely repentant yet worthy.

Working through the "repentant yet worthy" process was quite a dramatic adventure. Yet it was the gateway to casting aside my previous understanding of God as an executor who punished me for my wrong doings. Unfortunately, at that time I was unaware of Nonna's peaceful relationship with her God, and therefore I failed to see her instructive example. But as I came to believe that I was a beloved child of God, I began to feel and know God's love for me; it was a pervasive gladdening of heart rendered by the unconditional love of a parent for His child. There are enough struggles we must bear: unrelenting physical pain or unrelenting emotional pain. Why pile feelings of burden, shame, and unworthiness on top? It is time to grab some courage and adopt a belief system similar to Nonna's; a never-ending embrace of love and comfort.

May you possess the courage to:
- Believe in the purity of your soul at this moment no matter what prior transgressions may have occurred.
- Believe in your goodness despite how others may have judged you.

CHAPTER 7

The Question of True Surrender

THE HUMANITIES BUILDING THAT HOUSED THE MOST OF THE classrooms at the Chalon campus of Mount Saint Mary's College was built into a hillside of the Santa Monica Mountains. The lower floor of the building served as a conference center. Ceiling to floor windows served as walls for three of the four sides of the large space, revealing a spectacular view of downtown Los Angeles to the east, Brentwood to the south, and the Pacific Ocean to the west. During my undergraduate years, I would frequently head to the empty conference center to study in the evenings. From that vantage I could spread my immense biochemistry book, molecular model parts, note cards, notebooks, pens, pencils and highlighters across a large table. The vista of lights from downtown, Brentwood and Santa Monica was energizing. I had secured refuge from the never-ending socializing of the all women's college dormitory. *Ahhh. Thank you God for this truly extraordinary study setting.*

En route one evening, the elevator door of the Humanities Building opened to the lower floor. A small, colorful advertisement posted on the bulletin board directly across from the opened elevator door caught my attention. I shifted the heavy backpack off my aching shoulder and set it on the ground. The large letters at the top of the ad read, "Medical Missionaries of Mary." The paragraph immediately below described a community of Catholic Sisters committed to delivering health care in regions of great need. *Could it be?* This community of Catholic Sisters and their mission was exactly the mission to which I believed God was calling me! I worked the push-pin loose to read the back of the card. Yes! It gave the name of the vocations director of the Medical Missionaries of Mary headquartered in the United States. I excitedly scrambled through the zippered pocket of my backpack for a pen and scribbled the Medical Missionaries of Mary vocation director's name and address on the corner of a class note. *So much for heading to my retreat location to avoid distraction! Lisa! This is the life direction for which you have been praying!*

The Medical Missionaries of Mary were Catholic nuns. *I* wanted to dedicate my life to God as a Catholic nun! Not only were the Medical Missionaries of Mary missionaries, they were *medical* missionaries! Not only were they medical missionaries, they were devoted to emulating Mary, the mother of Jesus! The surrendering, pure-hearted example of the Blessed Virgin Mary was an important influence in my own striving to formulate who I thought God was calling me to be as a young woman! I believed God gave me the intelligence, the passion for medicine, and the deep faith because He wanted me to be a medical missionary! With great eagerness, I wrote to the vocations director of the Medical Missionaries of Mary. The prompt response letter I received told more about the Medical Missionaries of Mary organization and mission. The Medical Missionaries of Mary had set up hospitals and community health centers in Uganda, Tanzania, Angola, Kenya, Malawi, and Ethiopia. They not only delivered health care, they also trained local residents how to implement health care programs and run the hospitals and community centers. The thrill of potential life fulfillment permeated my being. I had found how and where God wanted me to serve.

Counter to what I believed was my life path, as undergraduate education drew to an end and the medical school application process ensued, rheumatoid arthritis ravaged my body, leaving me devastatingly debilitated. I found that I had to shift my diminished energies to focus on surviving. Confined to bed, I lay there analyzing the recent course of events. *God, I thought you wanted me to be a Medical Missionary of Mary. I thought I had surrendered all to You. Had I not? I surrendered worldly desires for a single life devoted to You and serving those in need. Why, then, are my efforts to become a physician and a Medical Missionaries of Mary being thwarted by vicious and unrelenting rheumatoid arthritis?*

I was cut of the same testadura cloth of stubbornness as was Nonna. I set my will toward a goal and did not allow excuses or procrastination to cause me to fall short of the goal. It took a lot of drive to become a doctor, and I was prepared to give my all; so *nothing* would prevent me from achieving my goal.

In retrospect, I had to ask: Was I forcing my own will on God instead of truly surrendering myself to God's will? Did God need to literally freeze me in my tracks so that I could recognize where He was truly leading me? Not completing medical school was, and being honest with myself continues to be, one of my greatest tests of true surrender to God's will. At poignant points in my life, I was able to look back and recognize that I was truly where I needed to be, where *God* wanted me to be at that particular time. My unique mark on history would be absent if I had forged ahead blindly and recalcitrantly into where I thought I should be.

May you possess the courage to:
- Believe there is a plan of Good for all that unfolds in your life.
- Make a regular practice of taking three or more minutes to be still, feel the pulse within and verify whether you are on the right path for you.
- Recognize and follow the plan for your life.

Chapter 8

Spirituality & Healing

In 2000, Time Magazine devoted one entire issue to spirituality and healing. Incredibly, there have been more than one thousand studies examining the connection between spirituality, religion, and prayer, to healing and health. Pursuing the concept further I was fascinated to read books and articles authored by a doctor who reviewed and analyzed the breadth of results from his own and other studies.

Psychiatrist Harold George Koenig, M.D., is an Associate Professor of Psychiatry and Behavioral Sciences, and Assistant Professor of Medicine at Duke University Medical Center. He is also Director of the Study of Religion, Spirituality and Health at Duke University. In his book, *The Healing Power of Faith: Science Explores Medicine's Last Great Frontier*, Dr. Koenig explains the intrigue he and fellow psychiatrist Dr. David B. Larson had regarding the connection between religious involvement and better health. Dr. Larson, President of the National Institute for Healthcare Research, and Dr. Koenig set out to study over 500 elderly people who had been admitted to the hospital at Duke University. Individuals in the group self-reported their level of religious affiliation; the levels ranging from no affiliation at all, to an affiliation with one of a wide variety of religious denominations. After accounting for variables such as age, race, education, support systems, medical illness, and psychological health, Koenig and Larson were astounded by the results:

- People who attended church at least once a week were forty-three times less likely to have been admitted to the hospital that prior year than people who had attended church less often.
- Of the people who had been admitted to the hospital, those who attended church at least once a week averaged a length of hospitalization about fourteen days less than people who did not attend church services at least once a week. The average number of days was 10.6 for weekly churchgoers versus 24.8 days for the others, meaning that people who are religiously involved spend about half as many days in the hospital.

People in the study spoke of how they relied on various aspects of their faith: attending church services, reading the Bible, belief that Jesus Christ will give them strength, or that God will see them through. Koenig and Larson speculated from these deep testaments of faith that people derived great inner comfort and thus experienced less emotional stress from their illness, treatment, or hospitalization. More findings from the study:

- People who regularly attend church service, pray individually, and read the Bible are 40% less likely to have diastolic hypertension than those who seldom participate in these religious activities.
- People who attend religious services regularly may have stronger immune systems than their less religious counterparts. Those who never or rarely attend church or synagogue tend to have the highest levels of Interleukin-6 (IL-

6), a protein the body produces to stimulate the immune response, perhaps indicating an overactive immune system. For example, people with diabetes, depression, rheumatoid arthritis or cancer have higher levels of IL-6.

- The deeper a person's religious faith, the less likely he or she is to be crippled by depression during and after hospitalization for physical illness.

The results of the spirituality and healing research were not a surprise to me. I had heard the results of similar studies, albeit unofficial, many times from Nonna. In one story that stands out in my mind because of its miraculous attributes, Nonna explained that when my father, Pasquale, was a little boy he languished for weeks with rheumatic fever. Rheumatic fever in the late 1930s was often a death sentence for children. If the strep-type bacteria infection and accompanying high fever did not kill the child, the pathological damage done to the heart tissues and heart valves frequently proved to be lethal. In fact, rheumatic heart disease was the number one killer of children between 5 and 19 years of age at the time. The seriousness of Pasquale's illness did not escape Pasquale's parents and grandparents. Pasquale lay in his parents' bed in the upper flat where he lived with his mother (Nonna) and his father. Italian-speaking *Dottore Rizzo* (Doctor Rizzo) faithfully came to the home each day. The scrape of the *dottore's* heavy leather shoes could be heard as he climbed the steep, narrow wood stairs to the second floor flat to check on little Pasquale. Antibiotics would essentially curb the epidemic's ferocity and the deleterious aspects of rheumatic fever after World War II. Tragically for Pasquale, he had contracted rheumatic fever in the years before the widespread use of antibiotics. *Dottore Rizzo* could offer little more than a daily "I don't know the outcome..." prognosis and a somber "Let's hope he will pull through this." For days...leading into weeks... Pasquale lay in a fever-induced semi-conscious state.

Pasquale's grandparents (Nonna's parents Genaro and Giuseppina Rizzo) lived directly below where Pasquale laid, in the downstairs flat. As recounted in Chapter One, Giuseppina Rizzo was richly spiritual as a little girl, being visited by the Blessed Virgin Mary and her angelic entourage. Grandmother Giuseppina's spirituality had deepened in the decades since her divine encounter. Giuseppina took the *dottore's* "let's hope" to an active higher level. She had unwavering belief in prayer. She spent hour after hour sitting next to Pasquale's bed, fervently murmuring intercessory requests to the Blessed Virgin Mary: *Please. Let Pasquale wake. Make him be cured of rheumatic fever.* She wholly believed in God's merciful answer to prayer and even more – expected divine intercession to heal her precious grandson.

Many decades later, I visited my father in his Florida home where he wintered. It was a break from the bitter Michigan January, but even more, a precious opportunity to listen to the stories of his life. The morning Florida sun gloriously streamed through the kitchen window and kissed my face as I sat at his small breakfast table. I relayed the version of the rheumatic fever story Nonna told me to my father who was now in his seventies. He jumped in:

"You know…I was so sick I did not know a lot of what happened to me during that time. I felt ill and hot with fever. You know that experience when you are so ill that all you can do is sleep? At some point in your delirium you become aware of sounds and people around you and fight with all your might to wake up but can't? Well…I had this sense of mumbling and a presence over me. I tried as hard as I could to open my eyes. When I finally got them open…all I could see was a burnt yellow color…in a second my eyes would pull closed again. A long time would pass and I would have that same sensation of mumbling and a presence over me…I fought to make my eyes open…again only dark yellow could I see. After what may have been days, my eyes were able to focus on the mumbling presence…it was…it was…"

My father's voice cracked and he had to stop to take a deep

swallow. I dropped the piece of toasted panetone next to the dried fig on my breakfast plate. I faced my dad, hanging on his last phrase… waiting in anticipation for revelation. He took a deep breath.

"…it was your great-grandmother Rizzo. I could

see her, she was kneeling, elbows on the bed next to my side…and her hands, clutching her Rosary, were over me. She was praying over me:

"Padre Nostro
che sei nei cieli
sia santificato il tuo Nome
venga il tuo Regno
sia fatta la tua Volontà
come in cielo così in terra
dacci oggi il nostro pane
quotidiano rimetti a noi i nostri debiti
come noi li rimettiamo ai nostri debitori
non c'indurre in tentazione ma liberaci dal male
Cosi sia

Ave Maria, piena di grazia,
il Signore è con te.
Tu sei benedetta fra le donne
e benedetto è il frutto del tuo seno, Gesù.
Santa Maria, Madre di Dio,
prega per noi peccatori,
adesso e nell'ora della nostra morte.
Cosi sia…"

(Our Father, Who art in heaven
Hallowed be Thy Name
Thy Kingdom come
Thy Will be done,
on earth as it is in Heaven.
Give us this day our daily bread
And forgive us our trespasses
as we forgive those who trespass against us
And lead us not into temptation
but deliver us from evil.
Amen.

Hail Mary, full of grace,
the Lord is with thee;
blessed art thou among women,
and blessed is the fruit of thy womb, Jesus.
Holy Mary, Mother of God,
pray for us sinners,
now and at the hour of our death.
Amen.)

My father's voice started to crack again.

"You know...she was saying the Rosary in Italian. My eyes would flit open only for a few seconds...probably several hours apart. But any time I could focus, there was my grandmother, praying over me. And obviously her prayers worked."

I was stunned. By all statistics my father should be dead. The rheumatic fever had left some scars; a heart murmur discovered during a physical examination after being drafted into the armed services. Yet here he sat, seventy years later, attesting to his conviction that it was by his grandmother's prayers and deep spiritual belief in healing that he had been spared. While growing up I had watched him doing hard physical labor or play on a softball league well into his 40s. I had jogged next to him several nights a week and had funny downhill skiing mishaps with him while I was a teenager. It was incredible, nothing short of incredible, as I thought of great-grandmother Rizzo's conviction so many years ago, and all the physical health and activity my father enjoyed throughout his life.

"Dad...that story is absolutely amazing. You need to write it down. You need to tell all your children and grandchildren! It is a remarkable story of how sincere belief and the power of prayer led to your full recovery."

My father's eyes had filled with tears at the end of the story. As I was encouraging him to tell his progeny this story, his tears vanished. He cleared his throat:

"I have more stories about great-grandmother's healing prayers. When I was a little older I was hopping barbwire fences with some neighborhood friends. The fences were six feet high, you know.

44

Well, when I hopped one of the fences, my shirt got caught in the barbs. My shirt trapped my arms, and I was unable to brace myself. The full force of my six foot free-fall was abruptly broken by my chest."

"Dad!" I gasped. *Oh boy! Dad must have given great-grandmother and Nonna some pretty hefty prayer challenges with his boyhood adventures…*

"What?" he responded with a boyishly-guilty chuckle.

"Well… after I fell, I had these two large lumps, like about this big…on each side of sternum."

He cupped his hands as if each was holding a half-pounder hamburger patty.

"The doctor looked at them and thought they were tumors. I was old enough to know that was bad. I thought…*Oh jeez…now what is going to happen to me?* But there was my grandmother. She made me take off my shirt. She placed her hands over both of the masses, closed her eyes, and started praying. I knew the traditional Catholic prayers in Italian, the *Padre Nostro*, and the *Ave Maria*, but she was not saying any prayer I recognized. She just kept on praying… really intensely…with her hands on the lumps the whole time. I started to feel this heat coming out of the palms of her hands. Then the heat started transferring to the lumps. It was really eerie, you know? And then the lumps went away."

Again tears came to my father's eyes.

"Her faith…her prayers…they were really special. She was really special."

At this point he stopped talking. Not because he had nothing more to share, but because he was ready to break into sobs. He wiped his eyes and nose with his breakfast napkin. My stepmother and I silently nodded in agreement; in reverent awe of my father's real-life spiritual healing experience that we had just relived.

Similar to the faith-filled people in the spirituality and healing studies, and the same as my great-grandmother, Nonna and father, I believed God was good and protecting and loving. But as you know, I did not always perceive God as unconditionally loving and benevolent. What could bring about such a monumental adjustment to my understanding and belief? It was Nonna's example. I observed and heard how she lived through numerous challenging experiences with her positive attitude, wholly convinced that God would take care of her in every situation. In Nonna's life, God comforted and protected without limits, even though the thought of such an unconditional relationship of love and generosity from God to humans was uncommon at that time. Today, the memory of her strength inspires me to go within and wholly trust my own relationship with God. I believe the powerful assurances I have felt from the Great Comforter throughout the years have saved me from the depression that often times accompanies chronic pain and disease.

In my life, I have put the phenomenal inner strength derived from whom I know as the Great Protector to good use. In 2000 I went to the Ann Arbor University of Michigan Hospital, alone, for my fourth knee replacement surgery. My friends and family were praying for me. I prayed with them, not merely for successful surgery, but also for the wisdom and guidance of surgeons, anesthesiologists and nurses.

In the predawn hours, as I was escorted to the pre-op area, the hospital corridors were mostly empty. The unnatural brightness from the overhead fluorescent lights reflecting back onto the shiny white floor tile added to the supernatural sensation I felt of being thoroughly uplifted. I had heard the religious term "uplifted" before, but thought it was a figurative term. Yet in those moments of heading step by step closer to the scalpel, I felt as if my feet were not touching the ground. Rather, I sensed I was being carried in the palm of a Divine Protector's hand, complete with the white fluffy clouds of heaven. I completely forgot about the pain associated with stepping on the worn-out artificial knee prosthesis, that while it had served me well for a decade, was now grinding and slipping-out of place despite its best efforts. It was about to be removed by the surgeon and retired into some orange-bagged, hazardous waste pile. I had no fear. Calm enveloped my entire being. I visualized the strong hand of Jesus on my shoulder as we walked side-by-side down the long hospital corridor; an indescribable assurance surrounded every part of me. The same permeating calm remained as I was wheeled into the operating room where the light blue-capped nurses, anesthesiologist and surgeons busily made final pre-op preparations.

Before the anesthesia took full effect, I pictured Jesus standing at my shoulder. I felt His strong grasp, reassuring me, feeding me strength, infusing peace. I had asked my family and close friends to join me in visualizing Jesus' presence and protection at the time I would have surgery. I pictured an angel next to the anesthesiologist and placed one at the side of each nurse in the operating room. And to my surgeon and the surgical resident I visualized the flame of the Holy Spirit over their heads. Oh yes…I almost forgot. I silently called the spirit of my mother to enter the room. *Mom, as you did when I was a child, look after me now while I cannot look after myself.* With a slight sigh I released any need to control or to worry and let peace and trust be infused throughout my entire being. Thus was my peaceful entry into the deep unconsciousness of anesthesia. The network of prayers and Divine placement in the operating room brought such peace and triumph to the surgery; I eagerly called upon it for the **nine** additional major surgeries in the succeeding years.

May you possess the courage to:

- Find peace, comfort and healing in your belief system.
- Find peace, comfort and healing from the thoughts and prayers of others.
- Call on the Holy Spirit or the White Light to surround and guide your doctor and medical professionals.
- Visualize a Divine Protector, Jesus or the Holy Spirit beside you or holding you.
- Call on your Divine Protector when your burden is heavy.
- Feel the assurance of a Divine Protector's presence.
- Feel the warmth of peace infuse your body as you release your health concerns to God.

CHAPTER 9

Letting Go, Letting God, and Resiliency

AMY AND I ENTERED DOMINICAN HIGH SCHOOL AT THE SAME TIME. It was a twenty minute commute from our homes in St. Clair Shores to the Catholic school for girls in the City of Detroit, and Amy and I grew to be best friends. It was not merely the time spent commuting that solidified our friendship. Amy's parents were divorced at a time when divorce was virtually unheard of in our Catholic circles. Amy listened and advised me as my own parents quietly divorced. As far as we knew we were the only two girls in our Catholic high school whose parents had divorced. By fate we shared that similarity. We also shared similar inner strength and move-forward attitudes. We supported each other through the emotional struggles that teenagers of divorced parents experience, and through our less important, but equally traumatic, crushes on boys from the two surrounding Catholic all-boy schools.

Long after high school graduation, Amy continued to wholeheartedly support me through my rheumatoid arthritis diagnosis, and my disappointment at having to continually postpone entry into medical school. The same enthusiasm and pep she exhibited during her Dominican cheerleading years followed into our adult years. Oh, how I admired her boundless energy! She resembled the wholesome, sultry Susan Sarandon. And yes, as I would tease her, she was her own local media star; she appeared in Grosse Pointe, Michigan's daily early morning cable television workout show, doing aerobic exercise in perfect time with the show's host. Amy was an advertising representative for *Vogue* magazine, was raising two athletic children, and helped out with her husband's general contracting business. Despite her hectic schedule she still had time to be my unofficial, but much needed, fashion and beauty consultant. I admired her ever-positive attitude and her unbelievably strong physical constitution. So you can imagine the mind-numbing shock I felt when I heard her say,

"Gig, I've got breast cancer."

An unremarkable occasion had precipitated the call. I had sent Amy an email, asking if she wanted to celebrate her 45th birthday by seeing the newly released *The Devil Wears Prada* movie. Amy was, after all, one of the survivors of the treacherous fashion magazine world. Amy's email was:

"Gig, give me a call. I've got something to tell that does not lend itself to email."

We did meet that weekend. We laughed through *Prada* and then had some heavy, soul-revealing conversation at dinner. I was amazed at Amy's emotional strength and positive attitude, even though she had to cope with the diagnosis of breast cancer and was now facing an impending arduous course of treatment. Why was it that some people exhibit incredible resiliency, even when faced with life-threatening challenges?

I saw Amy a couple of months later along with a mutual high school friend, Martha. Amy was about halfway through her twelve weeks of radiation. She told Martha and me she was experiencing the fatigue that sometimes accompanies radiation therapy. Despite the daily radiation treatment and fatigue, Amy's positive attitude was unshakable. I thought about her resiliency for a week afterward, and then called her. I told Amy that her positive attitude and resiliency were inspiring. I asked her for the secret to remaining positive.

> "My secret Gig? I'll tell you my secret. Every morning after my radiation treatment, I pull out of the St. John Hospital oncology-radiation parking structure and I punch my CD player. The Beatles song, *Let it Be*, plays. I listen to the words…"

Amy's voice started to crack, and she paused to stop herself from crying before continuing.

> "I listen to the *Let it Be* lyrics and I am reminded that God has a plan for me; that breast cancer treatment is part of the plan and I need to let go of the rest."

My mind flew to its vast memory bank of song lyrics.

> *When I find myself in times of trouble*
> *Mother Mary comes to me*
> *Speaking words of wisdom*
> *Let it Be…*
> *And in my hour of darkness*
> *She is standing right in front of me…*
>
> *Let it be, let it be, let it be, let it be*
> *There will be an answer*
> *Let it be*

Amy explained that God had a purpose for every thing in her life and that having breast cancer had a purpose, too. She revealed to me that dealing with the reality of breast cancer opened her eyes to aspects of her life to which she had been oblivious for years but which needed attention. Without the wake-up call that the breast cancer diagnosis delivered, and her subsequent calling out to God for strength, Amy mused "I may have gone on for years in oblivion."

I could relate to Amy. Having to face a serious chronic illness and the sudden and untimely death of my mother, from a young age I had come to recognize the fragile and precious gift that life and health were. While others may view the tragic events of my early years as misfortune, I hold them as rare gifts. While I have struggled with letting go and letting God, it is tremendously healing for me to be liberated from torturous questions such as "Why me?" and "What is going to happen to me?" Instead, I rest in the tranquil freedom of knowing it all has purpose. Yes, Amy. Yes. Let it be.

May you possess the courage to:
- Believe in faith even when you are faced with the impossible.
- Recognize every piece of your life has a purpose and let be anxiety; allow warming peace in its place.
- Always, always **BELIEVE** in your healing and the healing of loved ones.

CHAPTER 10

Miracles and Hope

AFTER ARRIVING IN DETROIT IN 1918, NONNA'S PARENTS MOVED TO the Northeast section of the city. The neighborhood was inhabited entirely by first generation European immigrants. Two-story wood or brick flats crowded the neighborhood streets. Whole families occupied one floor and rented the other floor to boarders. Such was the living arrangement the Rizzo family paid for on Helen Street; they were boarders in another family's home between Mack Avenue and East Grand Boulevard.

In the upheaval of moving across an ocean to a foreign country whose language was equally foreign, Nonna's Catholic Sacrament of First Holy Communion had been forestalled. Finally, as she reached her teen years, it was time to receive religious instructions to prepare for receiving the Sacrament. Each week Nonna would walk the mile to classes: west on Mack Avenue, then north on Mount Elliot Street, arriving at Saint Bonaventure Church. A Capuchin monastery lay adjacent to the church. The Capuchin Friars, clad in their long, coffee-brown wool robes, humbly ministered to the community through the church and monastery. The brown monastic robes were made by the Capuchin brothers themselves at the monastery. So, too, did the Friars weave the white cotton cord (called a *cincture*) that they each tied around their waists over the robe to symbolize their solemn vows of chastity, poverty, and loyalty. A large brown wood rosary was also part of their religious garb. The beads of the rosary were uncommonly large; the size of marbles. Five decades of beads (meaning five groups of ten beads each) were strung along the rosary, and ended with a single, plain, handcrafted wood cross.

One winter evening, as Nonna made her way to Communion instructions at the monastery, she was curious about a particular Capuchin friar. Would she see him tonight? She walked north on Mount Elliot toward Saint Bonaventure. Keeping her face down, buried against the biting winter elements, she glanced briefly to her right. Hundreds of grey headstones somberly peeked from the snow-covered cemetery. As a harsh blast of chilled air forced her back into her huddled position, she barely looked up; it was only enough for her to see a short distance in front of her snow-covered and worn shoes. The large steeple of the monastery appeared in the darkened sky. Nonna looked to the left for the cement path that would lead her perpendicularly from the Mount Elliot sidewalk into the monastery. From there she could see him. The folds of his long robes were whipped by the bitter wind against his tall, thin silhouette. The white snow, wild and horizontal from the force of the wind gusting off the Detroit River, gathered on and contrasted against his brown robes. Again and again, Brother Solanus stooped to dig his shovel into the wet, white powder, and scooped up a heavy load of snow to reveal the path to the monastery. Ignoring the bitter wind, Nonna watched as he dutifully cleared the path so that she and others could pass safely and enter the monastery.

"Oh, the poor man. He must be so cold. Only in his robes. Outside for so long."

With head kept bent to the ground, she passed the tall, thin Brother. *Ohhhh!* She was aghast. Her eyes still looking toward the ground, she noticed that open sandals were the only covering on the Brother's feet. As it was at that time, the Capuchin Friars also made their own sandals. Essentially, only four pieces of hard leather were used in their construction. The brown leather was in one-inch wide, quarter-inch thick pieces. One piece came across the toes, two pieces crisscrossed over the top of the foot and the remaining piece came around the back of the heel. Leather formed the bottom sole. It was not until the 1950s and 1960s that the Brothers started using old tires to form the soles of their sandals. In any event, the essentially open-footed Capuchin sandal was definitely not suited for Michigan winters. Nonna's big, dark eyes stared agape as she passed the Brother. She felt sorry for the monk as snow filled every open space between the sparse sandal straps, totally encasing his bare feet. Decades later, the vision remained vivid in her memory. Each time she told me the story she would shake her head in sorrow and click her tongue against the back of her front teeth in horror.

Nonna had heard the stirrings in her neighborhood of special "favors" granted to people when Father Solanus had interceded in prayer on their behalf. Miracles were not strange to Nonna. Remember, Nonna's own mother had witnessed a miracle.

The sixth child born to parents with sixteen children, "Barney" often missed elementary and secondary school to help out at home and on the farm in Wisconsin. In 1891, at the age of 21, Barney Casey entered the Seminary at St. Francis de Sales High School in Wisconsin. Barney struggled academically. After four difficult years of seminary, his school superiors dismissed him. Disappointed but not discouraged, he traveled to Detroit, Michigan, to the Capuchin Order at St. Bonaventure Monastery. He was invested as a Capuchin novice and was given the name Brother Francis Solanus. With his whole soul, Solanus wanted to become a priest, but the question of his poor academic abilities again plagued him. So fervent and committed to God was Solanus that his Capuchin superiors eventually allowed him to be ordained.

His ordination, however, was only as a "simplex priest" on condition that he never preach doctrine, never hear confession, and never grant absolution.

In 1904 he received his first assignment, to serve at a church in New York. He was given menial duties not ordinarily given to a priest. He cared for priestly vestments, sacred vessels and the altar. Returning some time later to St. Bonaventure in Detroit, Father Solanus became the humble doorman of the monastery, the "porter" in monastic terms, at which he served for two decades. It was in the late 1920s and early 1930s that Nonna would observe the simple monk about his other doorman duties: sweeping the floors in the long hallways of the monastery.

Nonna noticed that many people would flock to speak to Father Solanus, their faces stressed with desperation and urgency. The word was spreading that Father Solanus had the gift of healing and prophecy. No matter how busy or how tired, Father Solanus would listen, his piercing blue eyes meeting theirs, with compassion, leaving the plaintiff with a sense of peace that their plight had been heard and that this pure, holy man would intercede. Nonna heard that a desperate father had sought out Father Solanus to pray for his son who had been in the hospital and in a coma for sixteen days, fourteen of those days beleaguered by fever. The doctors had told the father to go home and make arrangements for the child's death and funeral. At once Father Solanus went with the father to Providence Hospital where he laid his hands on the child and prayed. After he finished his prayer, Father Solanus looked at the father and told him not to worry, that his son would be better by the next day. Another prophecy that became true. Within a few hours the boy's fever broke. Another healing miracle. Within twenty-four hours the boy awakened from his coma.

"Will my wife get well?"

"Can you help me find a job during these Depression times?"

"I beg you to pray for the protection of my son at his World War II station in Europe!"

Such were the pleadings of so many who asked Father

Solanus for his intercession for healing and prophecy. Father Solanus worked sixteen hours a day and filled seven notebooks with the more than 6,000 intercessions he had asked for on behalf of others. Father Solanus worked tirelessly, often to the detriment of his own health.

Inevitably, when Nonna told someone she had been in the presence of Father Solanus, that person would have their own story of healing or miracle or prophecy. Nonna's across-the-street neighbors, Mary and Don, knew the woman who had an inoperable brain tumor. The doctor told her there was nothing left to do. The woman and her husband went to Father Solanus at St. Bonaventure. After hearing her story, Father Solanus said,

> "Don't worry, don't worry. When you go back to the doctor you will see that the tumor is gone and you will have been cured."

Remarkably, when the woman returned to the doctor he could find no tumor! The doctor asked what had happened and the cured woman told him Father Solanus had prayed for her and predicted the miracle. The inoperable brain tumor miracle story was one I was assured to hear each time neighbor Mary stopped over for a visit when she spotted my car in front of Nonna's house.

In fact I heard countless stories about the miracles attributed to Father Solanus throughout my life. Nonna often spoke of the irony that it was not the high-speaking theologians in the monastery to whom people in need were flocking, whose intercession produced miracles, who were heralded as possible saints. Rather, people turned to a simple man who performed the humblest of duties at the monastery, who was forbidden from preaching doctrine; they beseeched this man who was supposed to be of inferior intellectual capability. Nonna just knew that it was from the humble simplicity and conviction of his soul that Father Solanus would pray for the needs and requests of others; this was the key to the success of his intercession. Every time she spoke of it to me, I could only shake my head in agreement.

From as far back as I can recall Nonna kept a photo of Father Solanus on the wall behind the rust-colored velour easy chair that was "her place" in the front room of her home. Framed in a plain dark brown wood frame, the 8 inch by 10 inch photo stood guard above her head. Nonna and her sister Victoria also kept photos of Father Solanus close to their hearts – literally! The oval 1½ inch by 2 inch photo had his last words printed on the back, "I give my soul to Jesus Christ." With a speck of brown robe cloth that had been touched to his tomb, the photo was encased in clear plastic, and secured by delicate hand embroidering. As they advanced in years, Nonna and her sister Victoria required help dressing and undressing. To those of us who assisted them, their secret was revealed: the plastic-encased photo and relic was dutifully pinned inside their bras! After my diagnosis with rheumatoid arthritis and the severity of my condition became apparent, Nonna and Aunt Victoria gave me a scapular with Fr. Solanus' photo and relic strung on a brown ribbon to wear around my neck. Even though I was in my early twenties and living in California where my peers wore low cut tees and bikini tops, I wore the brown scapular. It did not matter that the thick brown ribbon could be seen from the neck of my shirt. Nonna believed in the miracles that had occurred as a result of Father Solanus' prayers. Aunt Vicki believed in the miracles that had occurred as a result of Father Solanus' prayers. They had lived and moved among Father Solanus and so many who experienced miracles. As I lived and moved among these believers of miracles I, too, became a believer in healing miracles.

Nonna connected with Father Solanus. Nonna and Father Solanus were both simple human beings. Yes, simple, but both of their souls brimmed with faith. Most importantly, both Father Solanus and Nonna shared a common spiritual theme – they both held a firm belief and confidence that God was good and God cared. As a novice with the Capuchin monks, Francis Solanus meditated on the Bible passage:

"Ask and it shall be given" (Matthew 7:7).

Tragedy claimed the lives of loved ones of Father Solanus. Two of his sisters died of diphtheria, two of his brothers died in a single car accident, and two of his cousins drowned in the Mississippi River. Yet his faith in God's goodness was unwavering. So was Nonna's belief through the challenges and tragedies she experienced: God was a benevolent God, present in her life to help her; always there for her to lean on.

There are too many studies and publications on the link between spirituality and healing for me to ignore that there is a connection. If nothing else, the belief in God's benevolence and the existence of miracles fosters hope. My dear friend Maureen Dyar was struggling with severe rheumatoid arthritis when we met at Aquinas College. It was 1979, two years before I would be diagnosed. Never ever would I, or could I, have imagined that I would share the same fate and so imminently. Maureen told me that her mother took her to visit shrines dedicated to holy, earthly people whose prayers appeared to produce healing miracles. One such shrine was St. Joseph Oratorio in Montreal, Canada. Maureen and her mother had silently marveled at the stacks of crutches, canes, and walkers hanging on the walls outside the Chapel of the Oratorio. These crutches, canes, and walkers were left by those who came and prayed, or were prayed for, and who, by miraculous healing, were able to leave without their ambulatory aids. Brother Andre, C.S.C., was another humble soul that lived and moved among many in the twentieth century with miracles being attributed to his intercessory prayer. For Maureen and her mother, surrounding themselves in the location where miracles had occurred brought hope that healing from Maureen's rheumatoid arthritis would also occur.

I believe that the fact that I continue to be alive is a miracle! I believe the fact that I can walk on my own and work full-time is an extraordinary miracle! And the miracles I have experienced bring hope to what health challenges may lie ahead! Miracles abound! We need only believe and keep watch for them…especially in unlikely places!

May you possess the courage to:
- Believe in miracles and hope.
- Believe you will experience a physical or emotional healing miracle.
- Believe your loved one will experience a physical or emotional healing miracle.
- Visit a shrine, light a candle, and in the stillness and sanctity, pour forth your joys, your concerns and your sorrows.

CHAPTER 11

Angels

Similar to many Midwest Catholic elementary schools in the late 1960s, St. Gertrude elementary school lay adjacent to the century-old St. Gertrude Catholic Church. The school's tan bricks formed a perfectly rectangular, two-story box: perfectly utilitarian with no element of embellishment, spare the plain dark cross centered over the two main entrance doors. Visible from the east side of the building was the choppy, blue-grey Lake St. Clair, adjoining our city of St. Clair Shores, Michigan with Windsor, Ontario, Canada.

We lived, of course, on St. Gertrude Street, a mere half block west of the St. Gertrude parish compound of church, convent, rectory, elementary school, and high school buildings. Small ranch-style brick houses had begun filling in the gaps of the older farm-type houses that sprinkled the land. Towering, stately poplar trees lined St. Gertrude Street, ruling over shorter, leafy oak and maple trees. An occasional birch, with thick white bark peeling away from its mother trunk, appeared as a reminder of her role in lore about the Native American canoe. My older brother Peter, younger sister Laura, and I, old enough to attend St. Gertrude elementary school, set forth by foot each morning for the "Catholic corner," walked home and back during lunchtime, and returned home by the same sidewalk each weekday afternoon. One such afternoon, after traversing the tree lined-street to our home, first-grader Laura gleefully announced to our mother:

> "Mom! There were pretty angels in the trees…on the way home from school today!"

Laura's tone, while delighted, was also matter-of-fact, as if she described seeing a neighbor and his dog along the way. My mother, a believer in the existence of angels, treated the occasion with similar matter-of-factness:

> "That is wonderful, Laura! Why don't you tell me about the angels? What did they look like? What were they doing while they were in the trees?"

Of course, I too believed in the existence of angels. Well, think about it. I was raised in a Catholic world where God existed in all things, where God directed the weather and the course of events. I lived on *Saint Gertrude* Street in *Saint Clair* Shores and was named after the compassionate *Saint Elizabeth of Hungary.* My perception of the world was distinct in that what non-Catholics may have interpreted as supernatural was in fact natural in my reality. When the sky turned cloudy and dark as we walked to noon Mass on Good Friday, I assumed God quite literally was setting the stage for the morbid events we were about to recall, just as He had done at Jesus' crucifixion two millennia before. Thus, when Laura described the angels she had seen, I had no doubt she truly had witnessed angels. I remember observing the conversation utterly fascinated, but wondering why I had not witnessed any angels in the trees on the same walk home that day. When I asked my mother why Laura had seen the angels and not me, my mother explained that angels always surrounded us. My mother added that sometimes a child's mind such as Laura's was more open to seeing celestial beings than an adult mind, which was too cluttered or polluted to see.

"I've got an idea, Laura. Why don't you draw pictures
of the angels you saw?"

My mother and I nonchalantly watched as she drew
first-grader pencil-and-crayon depictions of angels in stick-
like trees. My mother believed Laura had seen the angels.
Laura believed she had seen the angels. Despite feeling
disappointment from not witnessing an actual angel, I also
believed Laura.

To this day I have never witnessed the physical
manifestation of an angel as did my sister and great-
grandmother, Giuseppina. But I unquestionably have felt
their powerful presence. On several occasions in my life
when I was about to make a bad choice, or was in the
midst of a poor decision's dreadful result, I experienced an
otherwise unexplainable force pulling me in the direction of
safety. On a couple of those occasions I quickly realized the
narrow escape. A chill ran through my body. *How incredibly
potent, the presence that just protected me!* At times of torturous
indecision, I am convinced it was the Holy Spirit or similar
divinity in an unseen angel that gave me the guidance and
wisdom I needed.

Perhaps belief in feathery celestial beings is too far a
stretch for some. If so, then why not look for angels in the
people around us? Better not, why not be an angel yourself?

Father Sylvester Ryan had the same idea. Father Ryan
presided over the Baccalaureate Mass at Mount St. Mary's
College in 1984. As we huddled in the chapel on the eve
of our graduation, Father Ryan delivered his sermon to the
graduating class. I recall how unsettled my initial reaction
was to the phrase he used as the premise for his sermon,
"Angels with Skin." But as he enthusiastically continued, I
became more and more inspired. The message of his "Angels
with Skin" sermon was that, as we prepared to depart the
educational enclave of Mount St. Mary's College to take on
the world, each one of us had the potential to be an angel
to others. I had long admired Father Ryan, his thick white
hair matching his broad white smile, and an Irish twinkle in
his blue eyes matching his Irish humor. But I was especially

impressed with his "Angels with Skin" sermon because it helped me to believe that being an angel with skin was an endeavor even I could accomplish – at twenty-three years old, with no money or possessions, no job and an arthritic body. I could be an angel with skin every day and make a difference, even while applying to medical schools or attending medical school. I thought I had to be a medical missionary doctor to make a positive difference, to be an angel among the sick and dying. Fr. Ryan helped me to understand that I did not have to be a doctor to be an "angel with skin." I was tremendously motivated by the "Angels with Skin" sermon. When he found me after graduation ceremonies and presented me with a copy of his sermon, I could only stare down at the clear plastic-covered sheets of typed paper, quickly glance at his face, and stare again at the words of his sermon. The words of the inspiring sermon, captured on paper, created a graduation gift so profound I have it in my possession until today, in its original clear plastic cover.

Even if you do not subscribe to a religion or believe in angels, you can do good deeds for others. Angels may not be the flowing-robed, feathery beings depicted in Renaissance art but rather the person who bestows an act of kindness upon another. Marla, who shared a dorm suite the first year at Mount Saint Mary's College, and her parents invited me into their home to celebrate the Passover ritual meal. During the beautiful celebration of religion and tradition, and in the years of philosophical discussions that followed, Marla's father, Dr. Monroe Richman, M.D., carefully and patiently explained the tenets of Jewish faith, many of which served as foundation for Catholic doctrine and practice. In a recent dialogue about God, Dr. Richman proposed, "God is a verb; alive in the acts we bestow on others." He and his son Keith, also a medical doctor, brought God alive to the thousands they bestowed charitable acts of medical care or advice. God is a verb; Monroe and Keith Richman are the angels with skin whose doctoring hands deliver compassionate action to people in need.

It is not difficult for me to see the angels with skin that

abound. Patti Paone was Director of the Mount St. Mary's Health Clinic when I worked there as a student health advocate. Patti and her husband Neil Posner appeared in my room during my stay in a nursing home. They were on a secret mission. Patti brought one of her dresses; it was one of those long cotton "bag" dresses of the 1980s—pretty much a one-size-fits-any-body garment. Patti and Neil had the entire mission plotted before entering my room. I had no idea! Patti was a nurse and knew nursing home protocol. They entered my room and quietly motioned to me the plan. Patti took the tent dress and easily slipped it over my head and hospital gown. Next, she gently fit my arms, stiff with arthritis and sore from the many plasmapheresis dialysis harpoons, through the arms of the dress. By the time I was disguised, Neil had a wheelchair behind me, ready to lift me into it. My room, being at the end of the hall, made it easier for these two to swiftly whirl me through the fire exit door undetected! The air smelled sweet...free of the heavy nursing home stench! The Southern California sky was dazzling to eyes that had grown unaccustomed to the natural light of the outdoors; I had to blink repeatedly before my eyes were able to adjust. Two street corners away from the nursing home was a pub. Two sets of curbs and I was in! I do not remember what I ate but I remember it was not the assorted pureed blobs of unidentifiably matter that was my usual fare in the nursing home. Patti's ever funny, ever witty stories made me laugh from the belly. Neil radiated his eternal warmth and joy to me. I eventually had to return to my nursing home bed but not before being filled with pub grub, laughter and warmth. It did not matter to the angelic quality or authenticity that Patti was Catholic and Neil was Jewish. Nor was the angelic quality tarnished by violating nursing home rules. What mattered was their act of kindness. Yes, they were angels disguised as undercover agents in a well-devised secret mission.

Each act of kindness and generosity that has graced my life, I believe, has been the touch of an angel. From the personal notes and messages of dear ones making me believe I was the most special person in the whole world, to those dear ones who have driven me and my ambulation devices everywhere! You are angels to me! And for the hundreds of people who have said prayers for me; you are all angels to me.

I have witnessed that every one of my angels, in the midst of their acts of kindness, no matter how tedious or uncomfortable, have been blessed with an inner sense of fulfillment or happiness. I know for myself, when I am doing a good act for another, in that instant I am not thinking of myself, my aches or my problems. Angelic acts, for as much love and assistance they bring to others, also reap peace and happiness to the angel with skin!

May you possess the courage to:
- Believe in angels.
- Be an angel with skin.
- Feel the touch of an angel.
- Visualize an angel beside you, with its arm around your loved one, or guarding your hospital bed.

CHAPTER 12

Caregiver Prayer

The GENEROUS HUMAN ANGEL MAY FEEL A SENSE OF FULFILLMENT and a charge of encouragement at bestowing acts of kindness. The caregiver for a person who is battling cancer, the caregiver of a person with an unexpected short-term virulent disease, or the caregiver for the victim of a sudden, life-threatening accident may experience the adrenalin rush of heroic efforts to save their loved one. Supernatural strength appears and aids the caregiver through lack of sleep, emotional battering, or bloody, messy caretaking as never before encountered. Family, friends, and the community rally around the caregiver with swells of emotional, physical and spiritual help. Over time, the afflicted person is either restored to health or dies. Most often, the efforts of the caregiver are focused on life-saving, last only a limited amount of time and, I don't mean this in a vulgar way, are seen as somewhat glamorous.

But what of the caregiver for a person who is chronically ill? For years and decades this caregiver may be required to suction phlegm or clean diarrhea whose characteristics are indescribable and obstinately difficult to remove from body, clothes and bedding. Their efforts are often met by irritated tones, and an unreasonable expectation of the person they are caring for. Few expressions of gratitude are forthcoming. Worse yet, or maybe not, there is no acknowledgement of any sort from a semi-conscious or cognitively impaired person. Calls from well-wishers and supporters no longer come. Gifts of meals and offers to run errands have expired. Prayers from the faith community have been replaced by new, more urgent prayer requests for others. How many husbands, wives, sons and daughters dutifully care for the person with whom they have spent a lifetime loving, but dementia has replaced with a stranger who is combative? These duty-bound caregivers precariously balance carrying out their own daily responsibilities with the need to provide 24 hour surveillance to their loved one. They are exhausted. Despite the caregiver's vigilance, car keys, medications and essential items disappear, tucked into hiding places by a loved one whose mind has lost its ability to recall. At the stealthy hands of those whose memories are severely diminished, stove burners are lit and left ignited, doors are unlocked and escapes into an unfamiliar world occur. The toils of a helping a person with chronic illness appears to the caregiver as never-ending. It is not at all glamorous, but rather is monotonous…tedious…hopeless.

In the late 1980's my friend Robert Stone presented me with two unwrapped presents. Both were small, short books on the prayers and writings of Mother Teresa. Robert was not Catholic, he was not even Christian. Robert had been Buddhist for most of his childhood and adult life. Robert had met me during the years I was not able to walk and it was necessary to use a wheelchair for all mobility. He knew of my genuine desire to become a medical missionary. Robert believed Mother Teresa's prayers and actions reflected the same prayers and actions of the current Dalai Lama, whose present incarnation was "compassion."

Another priceless gift: Robert packed up me and my wheelchair and drove us to the Masonic Temple in Los

Angeles to hear the Dalai Lama give a lecture, to receive the Dalai Lama's personal blessing, and to be presented a signed copy of his latest book: *Kindness, Clarity, and Insight*, the Fourteenth Dalai Lama, His Holiness Tenzin Gyatso. The Dalai Lama began his presentation by explaining his humble philosophy: the natural disasters, global conflicts and personal sufferings of the world…all could be overcome by compassion. The Dalai Lama pointed out that there were differing political and religious philosophies:

> "But what is of basic importance is compassion, love for others, concern for others' suffering, and reduction of selfishness. I feel that compassionate thought is the most precious thing there is."

A similar philosophy is apparent in the thoughts and prayers of Mother Teresa recorded in one of the books Robert gave me, *A Gift for God: Prayers and Meditations*, Mother Teresa of Calcutta. One prayer in particular caused a stirring within me. It described the exact disposition of spirit with which I hoped to serve others as a medical missionary and prayer formula for providing the strength to care for the sick:

> "Dearest Lord, may I see you today and every day in the person of your sick, and, whilst nursing them, minister unto you. Though you hide yourself behind the unattractive disguise of the irritable, the exacting, the unreasonable, may I still recognize you, and say: "Jesus, my patient, how sweet it is to serve you."

I wrote out this particular prayer and carried it with me through the following decades of my life. I have pulled it out at various crossroads; it always provides clarity and strength. I wish more than you know that I could tell Robert how much strength and clarity his gift has brought me throughout my life. Robert died of a hereditary heart condition shortly after presenting me with the gifts and the Dalai Lama visit; much too young in his mid-30s. He lived his short life as one of compassion and service to others, and I reaped the benefit of that example.

My favorite Mother Teresa prayer exuded purity and simplicity, yet her life was anything but simple. In 1927, at the age of 17, Mother Teresa answered what she referred to as her "first" call from God and joined a Catholic religious order called the Sisters of Loretto. The Irish community of nuns performed missionary works in Calcutta, India. Teresa found herself teaching the children of parents who had the financial means to afford private schooling in Calcutta. Within a few years Mother Teresa contracted tuberculosis, thereby ending her private school teaching career and making it necessary for her religious order to relocate her to Darjeeling, India for recuperation. It was during her ride to Darjeeling that Mother Teresa heard her second call, "the call within the call."

> "I was to leave the convent and work with the poor, living among them. It was an order. I knew where I belonged but I did not know how to get there."

The way revealed itself. In 1944 the Vatican granted Mother Teresa permission to leave the Order of the Sisters of Loretto. She was homeless and jobless, right in the midst of one of the world's most horrific slums. She remained a Catholic nun living outside a religious order and felt the weight of not knowing how to care for herself, much less than the multitudes of needy that surrounded her. In place of the habit of the Sisters of Loretto she adopted a white sari and head cover, similar to that of the Indian simple class. She ate only rice seasoned with salt, similar to the diet of the poor. She found a tiny wood shack and began teaching orphans or children of the unimaginably poor, even though the temperature inside reached 115 degrees and cockroaches regularly scampered across the floor. She encountered the sick and dying on the streets, rejected by hospitals. She held their disfigured hands, lifted their heads riddled with sores or rotted by leprosy, and spoke gently that God loved them. One encounter in particular was with a half dead woman she discovered in a pile of garbage. She sought care for the woman at a hospital, but the hospital refused to accept the woman. This marked a turning point in Mother Teresa's ministry of caring for the sick. She rented a room so she could bring in the homeless ill and care for them herself. Within a few years the Missionaries of Charity was established.

Mother Teresa's humble and selfless service led to a Nobel Peace Prize in 1979 and numerous incredible tours to meet with world leaders. We have all seen the pictures of her: the hands of Pope John Paul II on her bowed head as she received a Papal blessing; Princess Diana bending to hug her diminutive figure; her on-stage public chastisement of United States President Clinton and his wife for their pro-abortion policy. Here again we may be tempted to conclude that her service to others had a certain glamour. But in reality, the service for which she unwontedly gained global fame was in service to an unending number of smelly, worm-infested, destitute humans in whom she recognized the divine image of God. She sought and received strength in prayer and God's love. It was incredible that any human being could endure the enormity of need. Her faith garnered for her extraordinary sustenance. The number of orphans she took in grew weekly, no matter how many she was already caring for. Around every corner was a filthy, diseased or dying homeless person. Every day she was surrounded by filth, stench, and an insurmountable amount of homeless, starving, diseased and dying persons. Around 1948 and 1949 she began to experience spiritual desolation, an inability to feel God's presence. She described it as "darkness," a "continual longing for God" left unmet. This loss caused great pain within her heart.

In the book *Mother Teresa, Come Be My Light: The Private Writings of the "Saint of Calcutta"*, Editor Brian Kolodijchuk, M.C. describes the isolation Mother Teresa felt as she called out, "My God!"

There was no response from God. None. Merely a cold void and darkness. The recent public exposure of Mother Teresa's writing led to a global uproar and speculation that God had abandoned her, or that she was not the saint that many believed her to be. Extreme speculation manipulated Mother Teresa's experience of struggle to suggest God does not even exist. The speculation was far, far off base and missed the message completely. Throughout Mother Teresa's experience of spiritual desolation she continued to pray. She prayed continuously while she worked, in the few moments of privacy she had, and when she came together with her Sisters of Charity community. She prayed through the years of feeling as though God had stopped answering her. The intensity and frequency of her prayer remained fervent. It was through this incredible, persistent reliance on faith, patience and belief, that she achieved a soul-enriching, consciousness-raising result. She had a revelation...an understanding I can only call extraordinary for its selflessness. Her understanding was enlightened to see that perhaps she was to experience this spiritual desolation so she could to have a truly empathetic understanding of how it would be to live each day in desperate poverty, repulsive illness, without a shred of hope of being lifted, even for a moment, from the dismal existence. Can you think of anyone more empathetic than this woman who, with her own bare hands, cleaned the oozing wounds of a person would was going to die anyway and whom the rest of the world deemed inconsequential? No! Would you ever believe this woman needed to be stretched further in her spirituality? Not her! Yet it enriched her spirituality and empathy to be able to feel the loneliness and pain of calling out to God from the gutters of Calcutta and the depths of the soul, yet mercilessly hear no response. For the Calcutta destitute who prayed, the heavens did not open to drop an air conditioned, insect-free home with full pantry. For the dying person tossed into the rubbish pile, God did not respond to prayer with a flowing-robed angel that waved a wand to make the leprosy gouges or infected wounds disappear. Through her own experience of spiritual desolation, Mother Teresa realized she could relate to the spiritual pain of those for whom she cared, in addition to their disease, pain, and hunger pain.

You wanna' talk about courage? How about the figurative train load of courage it must have taken Mother Teresa to pray for the sick and poor, only to find literal trains pulling into Calcutta streaming forth even more who were sick, homeless, orphaned...her prayer seemingly not up to the challenge of the vastness of human suffering before her eyes! How about the courage it took to continue obeying God's original call to minister to the most desperate sick and poor, yet when she "dialed back" for some comfort and assurance on the progress of His project, God never seemed to answer her call? *Molto coraggio? Si!* Unquestionable Faith? Yes! Abandon prayer for others or for herself? Never! Mother Teresa never gave up prayer. It is even more critical to understand that Mother Teresa not only never gave up prayer, she continued a passion and love for prayer. Even throughout her years of spiritual desolation she encouraged others:

"Love to pray. Feel often during the day the need for prayer, and take trouble to pray. Prayer enlarges the heart until it is capable of containing God's gift of himself. Ask and seek, and your heart will grow big enough to receive him and keep him as your own."

Thus it is important to behold Mother Teresa's struggles and triumphs in seemingly endless caregiving to the sick and dying. Providing care for a person with long-term illness or disability can seem monotonous and exhausting. Providing long-term care to a person who is seemingly ungrateful or unable to express gratitude can dampen your spirit and be discouraging. The whole world may sigh and with sympathy say,

"Poor sick person! I will pray for him."

Nobody is saying,

"Bless that caregiver! I will pray for him."

No! The caregiver is often overlooked! Rare is the offering of sympathy or attending to the emotional and spiritual needs of the caregiver. So caregivers, on top of all the stinking unrewarded caregiving, in the moments of time you do not have to spare, I suggest you pray...pray hard. I offer the Mother Teresa prayer I pray when I want to ease myself into a change in view; pray it when you need a spiritual boost to accomplish the inhuman feat before you:

"Lord, give me this seeing faith; then my work will never be monotonous. I will ever find joy in humoring the fancies and gratifying the wishes of all poor suffers."

I call out another of Mother Teresa's prayers to help me when I am tired, irritated, or impatient with another. Whether in my personal life caring for someone ill, going through an emotionally tough stretch myself, or in my professional life when interacting with persons who are on public assistance, are partially physically disabled, mentally ill, or an incorrigible youth: I try to remember my vow to live my life as a vocation of service, no matter what the condition, disposition or socioeconomic status of the person with whom I am interacting. I force myself to bring my perspective back to the view of the daily task as vocation; an attitude adjustment that brings me peace and strength, and which consequently fosters a kinder and gentler action and interaction on my part. This prayer of Mother Teresa's is a jewel for transforming perspective too:

> "Sweetest Lord, make me appreciative of the dignity of my high vocation, and its many responsibilities. Never permit me to disgrace it by giving way to coldness, unkindness, or impatience."

May you possess the courage to:
- See your actions, requests, and situation from a caregiver's perspective.
- See a broken or dying person with eyes of compassion that compel love and nurturing.
- Pray your way through feelings that a caregiving task is insurmountable.
- Ask a caregiver, "... and how are *you*?"

CHAPTER 13

Bein' Right With God

Modern day confessionals are no longer the compartmentalized, dark closet whose floor-to-ceiling wall bore an opaque-screened opening through which you could utter your latest vexing shame. In most modern Catholic churches, you find an office-sized, well-lit room. Within the room you have two options: one of sitting next to the priest, side-by-side, concealed from one another by a fabric screen divider; the other of moving around the screen to a chair that allows you to sit face-to-face with the priest.

My 2007 New Year's spiritual resolution was to quit talking dirt about others. I never felt good about myself after the sessions of righteous tattle-telling or pot-stirring "snarking." It was an ugly part of me. And the ugliness smoldering within me felt as if a grey pall of ugliness had been cast over my outer appearance.

As part of my preparation for the Catholic Sacrament of Confirmation at the age of fourteen, I had to memorize the

Ten Commandments. I am not sure the list of "do nots" I memorized was the same as the list given to Moses or recorded in the Old Testament, nevertheless it was a list of behaviors you were banned from doing: "Though shalt not kill, Thou shalt not steal, Thou shalt not bear false witness..." I viewed these prohibitions as a way of "bein' right with God," even though they were phrased in the negative form. My knowledge of Catholic social justice teaching and Gospel readings also laid out the positive guide to "bein' right with God"...in the Beatitudes. The Book of Matthew described Jesus speaking to a gathering of people on a mountainside: "Blessed are they that mourn, for they will be comforted. Blessed are they who are merciful for they will be shown mercy. Blessed are the *clean of heart*, for they *will see God.*" It was this particular Beatitude: "Blessed are the *clean of heart*, for they *will see God.*" that I had used throughout my life as a guide for "bein' right with God," to assist me in hearing God's voice to direct me, comfort me, and love me. I envisioned a clean heart clearing the portal—*hwhah*—gently exhaling a breath of steam on the window to the heavens and taking the back of my arm, rubbing with my sleeve until the grime had cleared and the sound of squeaking signified I could now, finally, see God working in my life and in the lives of others.

It was with this "clean heart" Beatitude in mind that I prayed each morning, *God be within me...guide me in my words and actions.* "Bein' right with God" allowed me to start with a pure heart as my morning prayer implored God to fortify me with divine peace and joy. The super charge of divine disposition helped me throughout the day; in interactions with others to remain tranquil in the midst of stressful situations; to exude cheerfulness even when, as I stood talking to the person in front of me, I felt excruciating pain jabbing at several joints. It was "bein' right with God" that bolstered a loving and exuberant disposition. Yet I was aware as judgmental words were flicking off my tongue that it was not right. My critical words co-opted others and pulled them into the negative. My gossip hurt the person at center of the controversy. My righteous speech did not make me right with God.

I earnestly desired to banish the ugly-making part of me.

On December 31st of all days, a wicked winter storm threatened to coat all driving surfaces with up to an inch of no-traction ice. The Michigan State Police and Ingham County sheriff issued warnings to stay off all roads. The dangerous condition put to rest my wavering New Year's Eve party plans. I stayed home instead, alone, surrounded by Beethoven's Violin Concerto in D, clusters of lit candles, and entered into deep prayer and sincere goal-setting for the New Year.

> *Dear God, when I speak unkindly of others, it distracts from the peace and love I feel when I am close to you. Please help me see what it is inside of me that coerces me to find injustice, to feel prickling and agitation, and compels me to spread my thoughts and feelings through vicious talk. It is ugly Lord. I know it is ugly. I know it does a disservice to those who hear it from my lips. I know it hurts the person I speak against, whether directly or at some other spiritual level. Help me, God. I want to change so I can continue to bask in the soothing, enriching warmth I feel in my closeness to you.*

> *Is it envy? Is it because I believe myself superior? I cannot figure it out. Oh please help me! With Your grace, I will try to end the vicious talk. When a negative thought enters my mind, help me Lord, to keep my mind focused on the task before me. This year God, I promise you…I **will** cease my negative talk.*

My first day back to work was the third day of January. The TEST presented itself RIGHT BEFORE MY EYES!!! I could hear the alarm bell ringing in the back of my mind, the monotone recording alerting: "This is a test, Lisa. This is a test!" Did I pass the test, a mere sixty hours after my fervent pledge to God? No. Indeed, I practically tripped over my tongue as it started wagging and flapping away. I HADN'T EVEN MADE IT ONE HOUR at work before I began feeding the gossipy, sniping uglies!

*Okay. **Now** you did it. You wanted to do the right thing, but folded quickly and spread uncharitable ideas. Off to Confession for you!*

The Sacrament of Reconciliation in Catholic doctrine is a time to come to God with an open, honest and penitent heart. Sure, I came to God with an open, honest heart on a daily basis. I believed I was truly contrite and I earnestly wanted to change for the good. But there is nothing like having to face your pastor, admitting your uglies, to bring about sincere desire and motivation to change the behaviors of the past.

I arrived outside the confession rooms and saw that both Father Steve's and Father Dave's Confession rooms doors showed a red glowing light, signifying they were occupied. I had been looking to Father Steve for spiritual direction, but a family with several children was seated outside of his confessional. Father Steve's door opened, a child exited and her sister entered. The person in with Father Dave was taking awhile. Father Dave was the parish pastor. Maybe the person inside was also discussing parish business. *Maybe you should leave and come back when there isn't such a line-up for confession.*

I tried to fight my impatience. Heavens! I did not want to have to add impatience to the list I was about to confess. In my purse I had the rose quartz rosary beads Aunt Mary had made me with her loving, faithful hands. *It is the perfect time to say The Rosary...and maybe it will quell your impatience!*

Ah. It worked. I was already into the third decade of The Rosary when Father Dave's confessional door opened. I looked back at the mother of the family who were "ahead of me" in the line for Confession. She nodded her head toward two of her children as if to signify they were going next into Father Steve and that I should go to Father Dave if I wanted. I nodded back *Thanks. I will.*

I traipsed into the confessional, around the privacy screen, and plopped myself into the chair across from Father Dave.

"Hi Father Dave."

I uncoiled the fuzzy winter scarf I had wound around my neck and unzipped my thickly lined, black leather coat. I felt chilled driving to church in the frigid January weather and had not begun to thaw in the Confession waiting room. Yet one second in the Confession hot seat and I was already uncomfortably warm. I shifted my weight from one side to the other in order to sit on my hands. I *never* sat on my bent-up, painful arthritic hands. It was a dumb idea to sit on arthritic hands.

Oh my. You have reverted to the form of a Catholic elementary school kid; loaded with shame at the brink of being scolded. Quit it!

I jerked my hands from beneath my thighs and placed one atop the other in my lap, feigning a relaxed state. I looked down at the floor, trying to gather my thoughts, trying to figure out how to start my confession. I raised my head to face Father Dave. His head was tilted. He looked tired.

He has been listening to people's problems and confessions for almost an hour already. He is tired. Why should he listen to your silly problem? Just think up something that sounds like a more serious confession, state it quickly and let him get on to more important things.

Speaking very quickly, aided by my hand gestures, I told Father Dave about my New Year's spiritual resolution to stop saying unkind things about others. I confessed to him that my thoughts were critical and judgmental; my related actions were uncharitable and hurtful. I explained to Father Dave my belief that the negative thoughts and words detracted from the peace and love of God I felt when I rose above condemnation.

"I am here out of sincere contrition. I need to face you, admit to you these sins, to be as contrite as possible with God…so that God knows…He truly knows…that I will not engage in any further ugly actions."

I thought I was finished. Instead I added that a friend I had trusted had told untrue and unkind things about me to several others. I explained I was determined not to "return injury with injury" and that with fervent prayers by me and my loved ones – and the sheer grace of God – I had managed to not respond.

"Good," he remarked.

"The problem is…even though I believe not retaliating or even responding was the right thing to do… I now spend time tumbling around in my head the corrections I should have made to the false attacks. The thoughts are negative and even if brief…they are taking precious time away from my pleasant thoughts of God…time away from my continuous conversations with God."

When I stopped, Father Dave did not move on. My eyes were turned downward. A long paused ensued. When I looked up, he saw my hurt and repentance. I saw his compassion. He broke the silence with:

"Okay. What about penance?"

Since when did priests start asking us what penance **we** *wanted inflicted?*

I was expecting the usual procedure: "*Here is what I did that was bad…I am sorry for my sins…I swear I won't do it again.*" followed by the priestly assignment of a series of rosaries and Catholic prayers; and then the "God forgives you." blessing.

"I can pray for those who trespassed against me." *What? How did that come out of my lips? There is no way I can pray for them. The person who spread the untruths about me was wrong and hurt me! It would be too difficult to pray for that wrong-doer! How could I have just proffered, in front of a* **priest,** *infliction of the harshest penance on myself!* I quickly tried to backpedal and retract.

Father Dave's gaze was unblinking. The penance I had blurted was a most earnest and *effective* penance. I had uttered it on my own. And Father Dave was not going to accept any measure of backtracking I might offer.

"So let's talk about your prayer. As you begin your prayer…try to see the person as God sees the person."

I knew what Father Dave was asking. God probably saw some good in that person…or perhaps some struggle or hurt buried within that person. I also knew that what Father Dave had instructed meant I would have to try to see that good or unrevealed injury too…that was going to be difficult…I knew it.

"You will find when you pray for someone…so you see that person through the eyes God sees that person, very interesting things will happen." He paused. Father Dave repeated his revelation, word for word, this time with a slight, knowing smile. "You will find when you pray for someone, so you see that person through the eyes God sees that person, very interesting things happen."

Father Dave continued, "And the second part of your prayer...when you pray for the person, you ask God to help them in whatever their need is."

Oh, you mean I shouldn't tell God to make them realize how they were wrong, or to realize how much they hurt me? Directing God in prayer felt justified and necessary to make the other person realize their errant ways.

"Okay. How about saying an Act of Contrition?" He continued with the serious tone.

Uh oh! How did the prayer start? I dug through the "childhood-prayer-lessons" part of my brain hoping that if I could recall the first few words, my memory would kick in and lead me. I had been my nephews Ryan's and Michael's Confirmation sponsor only a few years prior and helped them memorize the Act of Contrition...why was it escaping me now? A laminated cheat sheet with the Act of Contrition was on the end table next to my chair. I found the version of the Act of Contrition that I had learned as a girl and recited it with full sincerity. Father Dave said:

"God forgives you. Now bow your head and I will say the prayer of Absolution."

I leaned forward, bowed my head, closed my eyes and opened my freshly cleaned-up heart to the blessing. I allowed the blessing to thoroughly fill me. It soothed and erased the shame I had placed between God and me. It gave me the conviction to not simply claim a quick and easy absolution; rather it gave me the conviction to never again turn back to the ugly-making actions. I also felt lighter. I was happier than I had been in the prior two weeks. The happiness lasted. Even better, when I returned to work the following Monday and the familiar opportunities for gossip arose, I chuckled inside: *No way. Can't hook me this time. Keeping my heart tidy now...*

I believe Confession, also known as Penance, has gotten a bad rap all these years. I had just experienced a beautiful Sacrament...freedom...encouragement...setting me right with God. Described as such, how does courage come into play with Reconciliation? Courage is called on in several ways. First, being right with God means you need to take an honest look at yourself. That does not mean you look at the other person and blame them for your feelings of agitation, your angry outbursts, or the recent drinking binge. No. Pull up some courage and take a realistic and responsible look at what it is inside of you that keeps you from being connected with divine peace…divine joy…divine love. While you are examining your thoughts, your feelings, and your actions, breathe in another dose of courage and look at the role your thoughts, your feelings, your actions played in situations. Did your thoughts fuel negative feelings…anger…envy… depression? Feelings that led **you** to falsely believe God was far, far away from your voice? Feelings of isolation from God – that no matter how far out you stretched your arms to be consoled – God's touch, God's warm love was not within reach?

Or did your thoughts lead to feeling the warm embrace of God's love?

And how about your actions? Did your words result in another person raising their voice in rebuttal…or becoming quiet and withdrawn? Did your actions spread cheer or raise morale?

For the next batch of courage you may have to bend down, grab each boot strap at the same time, and yank hard because you need to pull in a big load. True reconciliation means you not only want to change, but that with all sincerity you do change, taking steps to fight falling back to old patterns, sworn-off actions. "Bein' right with God" means becoming aware of whatever it is that keeps you from the close embrace of the divine, and making a brave and sincere effort to keep the path clear to all divine benefits: peace, joyfulness, and love.

May you possess the courage to:
- Be aware of and understand what distracts you from fully experiencing the embrace and benevolence of God.
- Free space in your soul presently occupied by the negative so it can be re-inhabited with the Divine.

Chapter 14

Prayer

Published scientific studies reveal how people who have active prayer lives experience less physical pain from their maladies than their counterparts who do not pray. The question of *how* prayer works to reduce pain is readily debated. A question of equal intrigue is: *how* does one pray?

Ask the question to a person who dutifully attends a weekly religious service and they might honestly answer that, while they believe they are faithful to God, their relationship with God is not conducive to a one-on-one conversation with the divine being.

Prayer is an intensely personal act. Prayer can take many forms. There is no *one* proper prayer protocol. St. Therese of Lisieux, also known as the "Little Flower," wrote a most beautiful description of what prayer was for her:

"For me, prayer is a surge of the heart; it is a simple look toward heaven, it is a cry of recognition and of love, embracing both trial and joy."

I believe prayer extends far beyond the recitation of memorized and recited verses. For me, the never-ending, daily conversation I have with God in the midst of living life, constitutes prayer.

People have confided in me they are not sure even how to start a conversation with God. During the religious formation of my childhood, much had been taught to me about what I could ask from God and what I should never dare to ask. Telling-off God and being foot-stomping angry because I was punished for tattling, even though my younger sister *had* chewed apart *my* paper doll, was a spiritual "no-no." Blatantly begging God to make *me* the winner of the piano being given away in a contest held by the local news station–because our family could not afford one with working keys–was not prayer. No, it was a selfish, materialistic act viewed by the divine as non-virtuous. More virtuous, I was taught, was to pray for the souls in purgatory even though as a kid I did not know any souls in purgatory. As a matter of fact, I did not even know what purgatory was, although it sounded dark and clammy, and somewhere I would never want to go.

As you know, Nonna helped me to see God as a kind, loving and benevolent God, not as a controlling, vindictive and punishing God. As a consequence, my relationship with God was one of revealing the joys, the struggles, the gratitude, and the questioning of mind and soul. In return from God I felt multiplied joy, comfort, and healing. I was no longer afraid to speak to God what was weighing on my heart. I was not intimidated to beseech God to assist me in my need. In prayer, I found the divine soothing of the soul that leads to the physical soothing of aching bones. When I awaken in pain, I try to first turn to a positive gratitude conversation with God:

> "Thank you God that I am alive today. Please help me with any physical struggles. Help me to know what you want me to do, give me the wisdom to know how to accomplish the deed, and the physical strength to achieve the task. Help me to be kind to everyone with whom I come in contact, even though I may be tired or grouchy because of pain or frustration."

Prayer is where I go in times of deepest pain. I may be overcome by frustration because I feel limited from pain or broken bones. I may be overwhelmed by excruciation in the hours and days following knee replacement surgery, rib-sawing thoracic surgery, or ankle fusion surgery. I may stumble upon a memory of my mother so endearing that it shoots a searing arrow of grief through my heart. In those desperate moments, I close my eyes and search for my divine connection. I bare my soul and divulge my fears, my hurts, and my needs. A brilliant light fills my mind despite eyelids remaining firmly closed. Warmth oozes into my being soothing the pain or fear or tension. I can almost hear a faint "Be Still and Know That I Am God." I linger on the sweet phrase, letting it play over and over in my mind. *Know, Lisa. K-n-o-w with every aspect of your being that I...am...your...God.* My mind singularly focuses on the "Know" and I "Know" my soul is linked with God. I am connected with my Divine Source and my soul is infused with the ultimate gifts of energy, peace and love. *Ahhhhhh...all is well.*

May you possess the courage to:
- Believe in prayer.
- Experience the potency of prayer.
- Practice prayer by whatever means connects you to the Divine Source.
- Spend three minutes each day focusing on the phrase, "Be Still and Know That I Am God."
- In times of pain or stress, close your eyes and repeat the phrase, "Be Still and Know That I Am God," until you sense illumination and feel the warmth of "Know."

Coraggio! Courage to Believe in Miracles

CHAPTER 15

Deeper Prayer

PRAYER IS CRITICALLY INTEGRAL TO MY ABILITY TO COPE WITH A PAIN
demon whose intent is to relentlessly jab and torment my
mind and soul. Prayer is so essentially vital to my ability to
have hope in the midst of a disease that daily finds new ways
to disfigure my body. When I saw an advertisement in my
church bulletin for a "Deeper Prayer" conference, I vowed to
attend. *Forget about the excuses you can come up with for why
you can't attend...make it happen!* Because prayer had brought
me sustaining hope and courage to succeed in living despite
chronic illness, "Deeper Prayer" sounded as if its rewards
would be even more successful.

The advertisement said "Deeper Prayer" would use the
spiritual exercises of St. Ignatius as a basis. *Let's see...what
do I remember about St. Ignatius?* The law school I attended,
University of Detroit School of Law, was founded and run by
the Society of Jesus, the religious order of Catholic priests
also known as Jesuits. St. Ignatius was the founder of

Societas Jesu or *Jesuit*, and thus I had St. Ignatius woven into my educational experience. I was embarrassed to admit that I could not recall many significant events of St. Ignatius' life so I did a quick online refresher before the conference. I was very glad I did the research because I learned details of Ignatius' life I had not known.

St. Ignatius, born in Loyola, Spain in 1491, became an officer in the Spanish army. In a battle against the French, a cannon ball ripped through the flesh of his left thigh and snapped the bone of his right shin in two. In the attempt to set his devastated limb, the bone that protruded was sawed off, and weights were employed with the hope that the bone would heal at even length to his right leg. As you can imagine, the unsanitary surgery without the use of anesthesia, the only surgery available in the 1400s, caused Ignatius of Loyola great suffering from pain, infection, and fever. It is purported that he fancied daydreaming about chivalry and winning the heart of a particular lady at court, but was instead given the only reading materials available: the lives of saints and the life of Jesus. Ignatius reported that daydreaming about chivalry did not satisfy his spirit, but reading and pondering the lives of saints brought him rejuvenation of spirit. This is the story of Ignatius' conversion. His spirituality continued to deepen while he was in Manresa, Spain. It was here that Ignatius recorded his experiences in what would become the book "Spiritual Exercises." St. Ignatius began using the practices outlined in "Spiritual Exercises" to teach others how to develop their knowing of, and connection to, God. Now, a little less than 600 years later, the participants in the "Deeper Prayer" conference would hear more about these same Ignatian practices and be invited to integrate them into their own prayer lives.

I am amazed there are so many people here...especially because it is right before Thanksgiving and Christmas, such a busy time of year! I counted almost one hundred people seated in the basement of St. Thomas Aquinas Church. *There must be so many others, like me, thirsting for a closer spiritual connection and sustained inner peace.*

Father Steve Mattson led a whole-hearted, thoughtful

opening prayer, beginning:

> "St. Ignatius of Loyola said God is laboring to love us. He is eager for us to open our hearts to let Him enter in. To help us open our hearts to God, St. Ignatius tells us 1) to Be Aware; 2) to Understand; and 3) to Act."

To help us understand the St. Ignatian way of prayer, Father Steve had us follow along with an outline from the book *Discernment of Spirits* by Timothy M. Gallagher, OMV. Here I paraphrase Father Steve's teaching:

> "What does St. Ignatius mean by "Be *Aware*?" He is talking about your spiritual awareness. He is prodding you to pay attention to what is stirring in your heart. In a moment I am going to have you read a passage from the Bible. I am going to ask you, 'What particular words or phrases jump out at you?' What reaction did you feel within you when these words jumped out?"

Father Steve was energetic. His voice was filled with excitement as he explained concepts and gave examples, some from his very own journal reflections written during an Ignatian prayer retreat he went on the previous summer. It was obvious he was passionate about practicing prayer in the way St. Ignatius found to be most fruitful in his *Spiritual Exercises*. It was clear that Father Steve's excitement was derived from the spiritual clarity and deepening prayer life he had harvested through Ignatian prayer.

> "Next, St. Ignatius wants you to *Understand* the stirrings you just identified...to help you hear what God is trying to say to you. Are the movements within you good? Do they bring you more connected to God...bring you to spiritual consolation? Or, as St. Ignatius points out, are the movements bad...do they move you to feel spiritually dry...farther from God? To help discern whether the movements are bad you may wish to ask yourself...What particular lies does the evil one want you to hear?"

Father Steve was touching familiar ground with me. For years I had practiced similar psychological exercises to help me become more psychologically aware...to recognize which triggers caused reactions of irritation, anxiety, and what situations brought me joy and fulfillment. How brilliant to apply a similar practice to spiritual awareness; discerning my inner movements and their effect on my spiritual state. Father Steve moved on to the third step in St. Ignatius' threefold paradigm:

> "In steps one and two, St. Ignatius gets us to discern spirits. Both of these steps lead us to action. St. Ignatius tells us to Act...to use what we have discerned from becoming spiritually aware and correctly interpreting our inner stirrings, and then to act on it. If the spiritual movement is of God, it is good; then accept it. Take action in the direction that God is leading you. Move forward toward God.
>
> "If the spiritual movement is not of God...if it leads us away from our faith, it is bad and must be resoundingly rejected. Reject the negative ideas that appear in your mind. Reject the negative when others falsely proclaim that God's love for you is not present. Act to reject any temptation that moves you backward...away from God; anything that creates a separation between you and God."

Father Steve then announced it was time for our first in-class exercise. He asked us to locate The Acathist Hymn handout. He started, and the entire class of one hundred joined in, reading aloud *Ode Four* of *The Hymn*. It was apparent that this was not a shy group, our voices resounded as together we recited the verses from Matthew 9:21-22:

> And she touched the fringe of his cloak, for she said to herself,
> "if I can only touch his cloak I shall be well again."
> Jesus turned round and saw her, and he said to her,
> "Courage, my daughter, your faith has restored you to health,"
> And from that moment the woman was well again.

Bam! That verse hit the bulls-eye on a raw spiritual wound within me. I thought of how much shame and unworthiness that Biblical phrase and related healing miracle passages had left me with.

Jesus, I know you. I believe in you so fervently. I can feel the stones grind into my swollen, crippled knees as I reverently kneel at the side of the dusty, hardened dirt road you tread. I hear the cries of the crushing crowd as you fi nally reach the spot where I have been kneeling... waiting...anticipating. I see the crude leather sandals on your feet as you pass before me, and I reach my hand out to grasp the hem of your robe. The forward momentum of my body and the swell of the crowd shove me forward and I feel my elbows grind into the dirt...but I am clutching your garment! You are so real! My fingers feel the coarseness of your woven brown robe! I know you will feel the passion of my faith...the depth of my belief that you can heal this infl amed, deformed body. I long to see your serene, loving face as it turns back...your compassionate eyes meeting mine, filling me with your restorative, healing light.

In my meditation, I knew Jesus so intimately that I could actually feel the coarse weave of his robe with my very own fingers as he walked along. But at the same time, I was not worthy of him knowing that it was me. My faith was not earnest enough to have him recognize the energy of my touch upon his robe. I was not worthy of him stopping his journey to turn around, crouch down, and with his powerful hands embracing my face, speak to me, "Courage, my daughter, your faith has restored you to health." No. I must have lacked the courage for true faith, a faith so genuine and unwavering if could manifest my healing. *A courage tough enough to...what was it? ...to move mountains?...or however that passage from Psalms read.* I had failed to have that kind of faith. I had worked and worked at purifying my heart and filling it with God. I prayed and prayed to be immersed so as to hear God and know God. But I was not worthy after all.

Oh, the shame. Oh, how the hurt is multiplied as I feel all those past experiences of spiritual shame rushing into my mind and heart...

Uh oh. I heard Father Steve talking again. My mind had wandered when I hit the robe-touching passage. During this time, the class had read aloud eight more paragraphs of *The Acathist Hymn.* Even though my lips were moving, my consciousness had spun off into a self-condemning examination of the unworthiness of my faith. Father Steve asked each one of us:

> "As we were reading together, what words took hold of you? I often ask people who come to me for spiritual direction, 'What was going on in your heart? What words created a stirring within you?'"

A woman many rows behind me said loudly:

> "Like the woman in the crowd, I reach out, knowing that you will make me whole."

A woman to my left spoke out:

> "O Jesus, heavenly Music, true Song of my Soul: You healed the woman who touched you."

Two men and another woman were brave enough to share passages that touched them, moved them in a healing way. It seemed as though the ninety-nine other people in the room had only positive, spiritual, healing reflections. But my stirrings were negative.

> *You think you are such a spiritual and positive person... yet at the first spiritual exercise you go negative on yourself. Your negativity cost you an opportunity to have a spiritual experience. You don't belong in this class.*

Just then I heard Father Steve remark that maybe...just maybe, some people in the class did not feel Jesus' healing flame of fire. Perhaps they had felt something else. He said to pay attention to that stirring, try to discern whether the movement was rather the evil one trying to dissuade us from spiritual progress toward God. I decided to tune out my negative self-talk.

At the end of the evening, I took with me the homework Father Steve assigned and vowed to adhere to the Ignatian prayer practices I was learning. Already, from only the first class, I had recognized a spiritual movement away from God and rejected it as St. Ignatius instructed. I was heartened after I rejected the bad and struggled onward. Had I not, I would have missed a soul-changing event.

In week number two of the "Deeper Prayer" class, Father Steve started by commenting on how he received complaint after complaint about his suggestion that we pray for an hour each day. Each person had a valid reason why they did not have a spare minute, much less a spare hour to pray. He also told of several people who said they awoke in the middle of the night or early in the morning. Father Steve said that when the Lord begins to speak to us, we may wake at odd hours, and we should take that as an invitation to pray.

I already started worrying about not being able to stay focused in prayer for an entire hour. But Father Steve explained how St. Ignatius believed in the Application of the Senses during the prayer. He explained further that there were specific steps for praying in "God's Presence." Father Steve was emphatic now:

> "Pray that God will behold you. Ask the Holy Spirit to speak to you, illumine you. Select a Bible passage and read it aloud. With your imagination, place yourself in that Biblical scene. Apply all your senses while you are in the Biblical scene: What do you smell? For example, pretend you are in the stable at the Nativity scene. *Sniff. Sniff.* What is that I smell... the stable animals?"

He chuckled at his own humor and the class chuckled with him.

> "What do you hear?"

> "What do you see?"

> "Speak to Him in your heart. He wants to hear your desire."

> "Listen to His voice. Is there a message He is trying to hand you?"

> *Hey, you've got a GREAT imagination. If the key ingredient in this type of prayer is your imagination, well, you could probably stay on track. Couple that with the sincere desire of your heart to feel and hear God and you may just be successful...*

Our "Deeper Prayer" week two homework was to pray

with selected verses from the Nativity passages of the Gospel according to Luke: Luke 2:1-14. I had tried reading aloud and meditating on all the assigned verses several nights in a row.

> *So all went to be enrolled, each to his own town.*
> *And Joseph too went up from Galilee from the town of Nazareth to Judea,*
> *to the city of David that is called Bethlehem,*
> *because he was of the house and family of David,*
> *to be enrolled with Mary, his betrothed, who was with child.*

Each night I only got about this far into the verses before I began to feel resistance within.

> *Why do I have to use the passages from Luke that Father Steve chose? The Nativity passages are used so often... worn out. The Luke passages that have always been closest to my heart are in the previous chapter. Maybe I should just move to the Annunciation, "Be It Done Unto Me" or Magnificat-Canticle of Mary,"My Soul Doth Magnify the Lord" passages and meditate on those...*

It was now Saturday night and I fell asleep without having finished my hour of Ignatian prayer. I woke up Sunday morning to my regular weekday 6:00AM time and realized I had already gone to the Saturday night vigil Mass.

> *Ahhh...you don't have to get up and rush around for once...mmmmm...time to cover your face, stay warm under the comforter and go back to sleep.*

A prodding inner voice offered a counter argument.

> *Remember what Father Steve said? Sometimes an early wake up is an invitation to pray. You have a unique opportunity to totally relax and pray. You do not have to worry about dropping off to sleep...or that you need to rush off. Just pray, Lisa. Just pray.*

I recollected the Nativity verses. This time I got past the first two verses without resistance. I moved along without the slightest distraction:

> While they were there, the time came for her to have her child,
> and she gave birth to her firstborn son.

She wrapped him in swaddling clothes and laid him in a manger,
because there was no room for them in the inn.
Now there were shepherds in that region living in the fields
and keeping the night watch over their flock.
The angel of the Lord appeared to them
and the glory of the Lord shone around them,
and they were struck with great fear.
The angel said to them, "Do not be afraid;
for behold, I proclaim to you good news of great joy that will be for all the people.
For today in the city of David
a savior has been born for you who is
Messiah and Lord.
And this will be a sign for you:
you will find an infant wrapped in swaddling clothes and lying in a manger."
And suddenly there was a multitude of the heavenly host with the angel,
praising God and saying:
"Glory to God in the highest
and on earth peace to those on whom his favor rests."

I began to engage the Application of the Senses part of Ignatian prayer and placed myself as an observer at the Nativity scene. My view was from a lofty position far above the stable, as is often depicted in Christmas cards. I looked around at the clear indigo sky studded with stars. Below, the faintly lit stable appeared tiny in comparison to the vastness of the night sky. I felt the chill of the cloudless night.

My gaze zoomed to the inside of the stable. I saw Mary first. She was kneeling, facing a small feeding trough. Although her off-white and rose-colored gown and pale blue veil covered her legs, it appeared as she had been in the kneeling position for so long that she now shifted her weight, so as to be sitting on her feet. The trough was lined with off-white cloths and covered with a light brown, woolen blanket. *Hmmm… The Baby Jesus must be cuddled within the blankets and cloths.* I could not see Jesus' face within the mounded bundle. I heard stirrings from stable animals, saw their back ends and felt the warmth of their bodies heating this place. Joseph was seated on the ground, at the opposite side of the trough from Mary.

I reminded myself, *Lisa, Father Steve gave you permission to enter the scene and interact.*

I stepped forward. *Voooom!* I felt pulled through a quivering time warp. It was if I had entered into another dimension– even though I did not realize it at the time. Immediately I assumed my usual Biblical "Martha" take-charge, helper role.

> *Oh Mary…up close I see you are merely a young girl. There was no nurse or mature woman to help you through the birthing process. Oh, child Mary! Are you okay, Mary? What about the afterbirth? And childbirth is a messy event…may I bring you cloths so you can freshen up? Childbirth is also physically exhausting. Mary, may I bring you some water?*

As I extend an earthen cup brimming with cool water toward her, I turn to Joseph and explain,

> *Mary needs plenty of water, and preferably more than just bread if she is to feed her baby. Do you have any food I can prepare and feed to her?*

I turn my attention toward Jesus. His rustic trough-crib looks different than the straw-filled manger depicted in the replica Christmas crèches I have seen.

> *Is Jesus warm enough? Hmmph…the irony of being born in the stable is that the warmth from the animals has heated your surroundings, Baby Jesus.*

I actually feel warmth from the crowded animals as I step in front of Mary and Joseph, to check whether the newborn feels warm. A force stops me. Simultaneously I recognize I am in the worry and control mode. I chastise myself:

> *Stop being such a Martha!*

I step back and notice that Mary and Joseph are gazing undisturbed in adoration of Baby Jesus. Their faces bore the expression of sweet contentment as they gazed unceasingly upon Jesus. They were not paying attention to my fussing. I realized that as I approached the place where Jesus lay, a soft golden glow and warmth radiated outward. I never actually saw a baby. In its place I saw light and I could actually feel the warmth of divine love. The warmth first touched my face, moved to my head, and then permeated my entire body. With the warmth came an incredible sensation of deep relaxation. I fought the desire to urgently seek medical attention for Mary. I railed against urging Joseph to flee because there were bad men on their way to hurt Mary and kill the newborn child. I became so awash with the wave of warm, divine love, I stopped the mind-babble mid-sentence. By letting go of the call to duty and ceasing my chatter, I was given the sacred space to feel what Mary and Joseph were feeling. I looked at their faces. *This is other-worldly!* No words were exchanged, yet I could feel their exact inner feelings. My mind was filled with everything held within their hearts. Their expression was,

> "We are living in this moment of perfect love. This moment of perfect gift of God's love. There is no worry that can displace the moment of perfect love."

The message that flowed to me was strong, clear and loud:

> *Lisa. There is no need to worry. God's love is present for you also. Of all the time and energy you spent in your lifetime steeped in anxiety and worry–God was always there–He took care of you. Always. Remember for the future, to forgo worry. The worry, the painfully anxious moments, they were all wasted time and energy. You have been given the gift of living in the present moment of God's love.*

My whole body felt warm…tranquilly warm. I could see a golden glow all around the stable emanating from Jesus and encircling everyone who was there, including me. It was the most incredible sensation; ethereal, yet very real. It was a feeling that thoroughly filled every aspect of my person, of being warm, being protected, being loved, and being nourished. With that feeling, I had a deep knowing that I would never have another worry, not ever, because the power of God was paramount. I wondered:

> *Is this what it feels like to see the Face of God?*

I wanted to gather the divine sensation safely into my

soul, to be stored eternally, so that I could summon it from within if needed, and experience it again and again…forever.

Wait! I have to know! Is this the all-encompassing love and warmth and glow that greeted Mom and Nagymama at the moments of their untimely deaths?

"YES. And their souls were overwhelmed with joy. They were completely enveloped in peace… and remain thus."

The voice delivering the message was deep, a resounding boom. I felt the air rush out of my lungs. It was if the tremendous burden I had been carrying around for twenty years had been expelled. The auto accident that caused my mother's and Nagymama's deaths was horrific…their deaths entirely unexpected. There had been no opportunity to resolve unfinished business, no opportunity to forgive, or to speak a final "I love you." I had strained myself with wonder:

Had their souls felt peace when they were received by God after such a violent thrust from this life? Were they entirely consumed with love, leaving all worry about unresolved matters behind?

I saw my mother's beautiful face before me now. Her eyes were peacefully closed and her face bore a blissful smile. Her face glowed with soft light. I felt my chest spasm as sobs of joy poured forth.

Yes! Oh thank you God. Mom felt this same overwhelming peace and love as she left this world and entered the next. She continues to bask in this glow and warmth. Oh thank you, God. Thank you, God!

Just then, a jolt ran from my mind through my body.

Wait! No. Please…NO!

I felt myself being pulled out of the warm cocoon of love… pulled back into my cold room. Pulled back into my own mind.

NOOOOOOO!!!!!!!

I heard my objections echo through my mind. It felt as if I was being furiously sucked backward through a cold vacuum, the pressure of the vacuum creating an echo chamber for my cry. I did not want to go yet! I did not want to leave this place of beautiful divine peace. I tried to force my mind back to the Nativity scene.

> *C'mon, concentrate! Get back there! C'mon, pray. Try harder.*

I pressed my eyelids together and scrunched my face tight. Yet no matter how hard I prayed, how long I prayed, I could not get back to that divine place of unknown time and space.

Surprisingly, I was not too disappointed in the retreat back to reality. For a time I was on a spiritual high. I wanted to write down every thought, every sensation and most importantly, every message from God. I forced myself to still my mind so that I could recall and hear the messages God had for me during my prayer experience.

Before I had read the Nativity passage and applied the senses with my imagination, I had asked God to give me clarity, perhaps some sign that I was supposed to be spending my non-work hours writing an inspirational book. For twenty years I had heard a call...I believed it from God...that there was a reason for experiencing crippling arthritis and paralyzing myasthenia gravis; a reason for the excruciating losses of mother and grandmother in the devastating highway accident. But the time taken to write detracted from time with loved ones or the pursuit of career advancements. In addition, although I had a highly-developed intuition, the ability to see the interconnectedness of the world, and keen, deep feelings, I stunk at putting that intuition, global insight, and my profound feelings into writing.

> *Surely if God intended you to write a book, He would have bestowed upon you talent for writing.*

I argued this valid point within myself endlessly.

Yet when, with mind quieted, I recollected the fantastic Nativity prayer experience, I was surprised that the question I posed to God... no, to be honest, the question I *demanded* that God answer for me, was not the focus of God's message. God's message was directed at a much deeper and more profound aspect of my soul: my gut-twisting, insomnia-provoking, multi-faceted anxiety and worry. I had been a worrywart from youth. As an adult, the emotional stranglehold that anxiety had over me continued, most likely spewing tons of hormones and toxins into my delicately balanced system; the lack of sleep from insomnia was absolutely brutal on my fragile body.

Thus, what was so very interesting to me at that moment was that I had not received an answer from God to the question I had verbalized: *am I to proceed with writing the book?* Instead, God spoke to me and literally moved through me with unearthly stirrings of love and peace, to assuage the oppressive, immobilizing, time and energy wasting anxiety, worry and upset. The very anxiety, worry, and upset that kept me from grasping the link to God's peace, God's joy, and God's love. God's tone was compassionate, perhaps with a hint of chiding:

"All that time wasted on worrying about a particular concern? Wasted. All the agitation you lived with because of some issue? Didn't change the outcome. Those many nights twisting in emotional torment? The palm of My hand was there too, you know, for you to find refuge and rest."

Because I could hear and feel God's message at the same time, it is difficult for me to express adequately how clearly and how thoroughly it communicated this to me:

"There is never, ever a need for worry. Worry is a waste of your earthly time. I will always ensure you are okay. I am allowing you to feel and taste how it is to live free, unhindered in my love and my peace. What I want for you is to let me embrace you with my peace and love…always. Anxiety is a barrier to the full flow of love I pour over you abundantly. Let go of anxiety, Lisa. Let me gently and wholly wrap you in my warm, eternal love."

Wow! This was a life-changing experience. Truly, every part of me felt changed. I was light. I was vibrant. I was rested. Challenges to my equanimity came at me quickly and furiously…it was astounding, absolutely astounding, how I was able to stop, recall and rely on those powerful words of love, and resist succumbing to an anxious reaction, to so easily let go of worry.

My friend Maura was as wise in making legal judgments as she was with spiritual insight. At dinner one night, I huddled over the table toward Maura so that the person in the adjoining restaurant booth could not hear. I told Maura of my profound disappointment that, although I believed myself to have faith as strong as the woman who touched Jesus' robe, I had not been healed of rheumatoid arthritis.

"So how do you know you have not been healed in other ways?" Maura asked.

I thought back on Maura's question. *Yes. You've received the healing touch of peace and love. And what a tremendous endowment: a healing that encompasses and intersects every facet of your life.*

There was another surprise to the "Deeper Prayer" conference experience. It was God's answer to my unspoken question of what happened to the souls of my mother and grandmother at the time of their unexpected deaths. Toward the end of the experience, when I melted in warmth and love, I uttered,

Ahhhh…is this how it feels to see the face of God?

The nagging question I carried with me since the first moments I heard the hospital volunteer on the other end of the phone line tell me my mother had been killed was, "What happened to Julia's beautiful soul?" Was there any truth to the Catholic doctrine of a dismal purgatory? I prayed and prayed for the escape of Mom's soul from the wretched place just in case. Was there any chance she was sentenced to Hell? Unfathomable. I cannot recount the number of times Mom and I debated whether reincarnation was a possible phenomenon. After her death the day before Christmas Eve 1986 however, I could not reconcile a reincarnation philosophy with my strong sense that Mom entered heaven in time to add her voice to the angelic Christmas choir.

God's surprising decree to me about His presence at the moments of Mom's and Nagymama's death was this:

> "YES, they are with Me. And their souls were overwhelmed with joy. They were completely enveloped in peace…and remain thus…"

Had I ever directly asked God about the well-being of their souls? I could not recall; it had been several years. But here, now, God had answered a decades-long, deeply troublesome question for me. Better than that, I had been reassured that their souls were met with a love...a peace...a joy that they never could have imagined in their earthly bodies and minds. I had felt the encompassing, warming love of God. I knew with certainty now. I no longer needed to worry that they suffered or were trapped in purgatory. Once again, Maura's prophecy rang in my memory. I had been healed of a long-standing, jabbing mystery. This time the unknowing had been resolved, and the answer was good... an all-encompassing Good.

Ironically, but maybe not so ironic, come to think of it, I have used my Deeper Prayer gift to reassure several grieving friends that the soul of their loved one is enraptured in a love beyond anything we can comprehend. And I speak with a genuine sense of knowing. I share my story as an affirmation of this knowing. Some people think I am a bit off, I am sure. I do not care. For I know and feel what I experienced. It was an experience that transcends anything we can know in this world; I will not make any excuse for it or withhold it.

It takes courage to enter into this deeper relationship with God. Father Steve warned us about it. St. Ignatius wrote about it. St. Ignatius preached that a critical part of being aware of and understanding the stirrings of your soul is to discern those who may be launched against you by the evil one, to be on guard against such evil prodding, and to reject them. Yes, I have had spiritual challenges come from all directions, but now I am wiser.

In the Lenten period following my profound spiritual experience of coming to know God's benevolent embrace, and hearing His voice more clearly through a deeper prayer practice, the Gospel readings from John told of Jesus' healing endeavors. He even raised His friend Lazarus from the dead. This time, as I heard and reflected on the Lenten scripture readings, I was not overcome by unworthiness or justified punishment, as in the past. Instead, I was struck by the message:

> As he passed by he saw a man blind from birth.
> His disciples asked him, "Rabbi, who sinned,

this man or his parents, that he was born blind?"

Jesus answered, *"Neither he nor his parents sinned;*

it is so that the works of God might be made visible through him.

We have to do the works of the one who sent me while it is day.

Night is coming when no one can work.

While I am in the world, I am the light of the world."

When he had said this, he spat on the ground and made clay with the saliva,

and smeared the clay on his eyes,

and said to him, "Go wash in the Pool of Siloam" (which means Sent).

So he went and washed, and came back able to see. (New American Bible. John 9:1-7. Italics added.)

See. The man's blindness was not God's punishment for sins this man had committed; nor was the man being punished by God for his parents' sins. God's benevolence restored his vision and the man, in turn, went forth to encourage others to believe in God's benevolence! This is a message for you, too. Do not despair. Reject the false assumption that your illnesses and physical limitations are punishment for sins. Instead, have Hope in God's Goodness. Believe so that you may open yourself to fully accept God's benevolence! And in whatever form the healings or messages come, accept them so you can go forth and encourage others!

At the same time as I was coming into a fuller realization of God's compassion, my Deeper Prayer partner, also named Lisa, gave me a prayer-mediation exercise from the book *An Ignatian Introduction to Prayer: Spiritual Reflections According to the Spiritual Exercises,* by Father Timothy M. Gallagher. I had confided in Lisa the self-condemnation I felt during the in-class exercise about the woman who touched Jesus' cloak and had been healed. Lisa avowed that this particular prayer-meditation was powerful. Later, alone in my quiet prayer space, I opened the pages and saw the New Testament story of Bartimaeus, the blind beggar, who was also healed through an encounter with Jesus.

Oh no. Another Jesus healing story.

Immediately, anxiety had seized me.

This is not going to be good. If you read this, you will only be reminded of how unworthy you are in the eyes of God. The evidence: **you** *have yet to be healed…*

*Stop! You have been given the gift of knowing God's all-encompassing love for you. You have been given the gift of feeling God's warm assurance that all is well, and all will be for the good in your life. Accept **this** as the truth, not this false conclusion.*

I opened my Bible and read the passages assigned in the book:

…as he was leaving Jericho with his disciples and a sizable crowd,
Bartimaeus, a blind man, the son of Timaeus, sat by the roadside begging.
 On hearing that it was Jesus of Nazareth, he began to cry out and say,
"Jesus, son of David, have pity on me."
And many rebuked him, telling him to be silent.
But he kept calling out all the more,
"Son of David, have pity on me."
Jesus stopped and said, "Call him."
So they called the blind man, saying to him,
"Take courage; get up, he is calling you."
He threw aside his cloak, sprang up, and came to Jesus.
Jesus said to him in reply, "What do you want me to do for you?"
The blind man replied to him, "Master, I want to see."
Jesus told him, "Go your way; your faith has saved you."
Immediately he received his sight and followed him

on the way.
(*New American Bible*. Mark 10:46-52. Italics added.)

I glanced over the Ignatian prayer-mediation exercises suggested for these passages and closed my eyes. Slowly and patiently I applied my senses to the Biblical scene: barren, parched, Asia Minor landscape.

My view panned in and I found myself at the side of a dusty, narrow dirt road. There are crowds of people lining each side of the road. They jostle against me, but it is as if I am invisible. Not one of them acknowledges my presence. Although the crowd is dressed in the tunics and sandals typical of biblical times, for some undecipherable reason I see myself in a hooded sweatshirt. It is a blue-grey pullover and the hood is pulled tightly over my head and face. It is so snug that it almost entirely covers my eyes. Both of my hands are stuffed into the front pouch pocket of the sweatshirt. I hear the crowd become agitated as Jesus approaches. I cannot see him through the throng but from the roar of the crowd, I assume Jesus is near.

I speak in an ordinary tone, without raising my voice,
"Jesus, son of David, have mercy on me."

There is no acknowledgement to my call. I repeat, "Jesus, son of David, have mercy on me," hearing only my own voice as the din of the crowd muffles my words. A couple of men turn around and, with gesticulating hands to underscore the urgency, they appeal to me:
"*He is calling **you**!*"
What? He is calling you? You doubted before that He even took notice of you before, even though you tightly grasped his robe. Now, through the clacking and jostling crowd, He has heard your passive plea...He has heeded your humble appeal and now beckons you to His side!

Entirely enveloped in the scene now, I see myself throw down my purse with all its contents; my wallet, my money, my cell phone, my day planner, my two tubes of lipstick, my contact lens rewetting solution–all the critical items of my world.

Are you kidding me? You abandon both tubes of lipstick?

*You must be losing it. You **never** allow yourself to be seen in public without lipstick, under eye cover and mascara! That Estee Lauder tube alone cost you over $20.00! Really…reconsider…after the great lengths you go to protect your finances…you can't just throw your credit cards into the hands of thieves!*

I pull my hands out of the sweatshirt pouch and discard the car keys that I had clutched in my right hand.

Oh no. Not your keys. Don't discard them! You can barely walk on your damaged ankles…you'll be sunk without your car…

I pull off the sweatshirt and drop it in the dirt at the side of the road.

I see myself in front of Jesus now. All I am wearing is a long, pure white cotton tunic. My face is scrubbed clean, not a shimmer of makeup to be found. My hair is combed straight; no bobby-pins, elastic bands or self-imposed curls. Just the bare me…soul scrubbed clean of malevolence, shame, and unworthiness…body and heart in purest form.

I stand face to face with Jesus, my soul wide open. We look each other in the eye. The intense Middle East sun beats down on us and illumines His amazing and penetrating eyes. I know He sees clearly through to my open soul. The noise of the crowd has vanished. Jesus speaks first:

"…what do you want me to do for you?"

*Ohhhh… what do I want **you** to do for **me**?????*

I start reciting my list. Unashamedly, never breaking eye contact. We stand there for what seemed hundreds of minutes.

Then abruptly, the prayer refl ection ended. I grabbed for my prayer journal…I realized I had just received another profound message:

"Just ask. All you ever had to do was talk to me. Just ask me…what do you want me to do for you?" Yes. To fully experience God's benevolence for you, only believe you can ask anything of Him. Believe that He will hear you. Cast aside whatever cloak may be a hindrance to your coming before Him, hands outstretched, soul wide-open…and ask. You know you will receive answer… as

you have here.

Did it take a whole bunch of courage for me to face my fears and reject other peoples' condemnation about unworthiness and divine retribution? *You 'betcha.* The judgmental pronouncements were heavy obstacles keeping me from experiencing a covenantal relationship with God, keeping me from a whole experience of God's self-revelation: God revealing Himself to me and me revealing myself to Him. The harvest reaped from the courageous rejection of negative edicts of others was a clear portal through which God could plainly see me in all my bodily and spiritual aspects, and I could see Him in all His aspects. And through that clear portal I discovered the reassuring message that God is there for me–always–whether or not I, or anyone else thinks I deserve it.

Did it take a whole bunch of courage for me to openly beg God's forgiveness, to forgive myself and to forgive others? *You 'betcha.* But it is in the act of earnest contrition, followed by the forgiveness of oneself and of others, that the healing balm of the Divine can soothe the deepest of wounds.

Did it take a whole lot of courage to be persistent in prayer, even though I had every rationalization and shred of evidence lined up to abandon my prayer conversation with God? *You 'betcha.* The grace to persevere, the grace to resist the temptation to abandon prayer, the grace to hold fast to my belief in God, has been life-changing. My whole being is fully permeated by the reassurance that is God working Good in my life. God is working Good in my life despite the pain. God is working Good in my life despite continued physical deterioration. With this enhanced understanding comes a heightened sense of eagerness to assist others to achieve divine assurance and hope. In this eagerness, I encourage you to refuse the negative judgments of others, or yourself, so that you may fully, and without obstacle, experience the pure, abundant relationship with the Source of Life, the Universe, Divine energy, God, or whatever you call the connection to the Life-giving force. Nonna's belief in the ever-benevolent Presence gave her the courage to step forward in faith to meet every occasion. In my moments of doubt, and believe me, I have doubts despite the enlightened assurance I have spoken of, I am reminded to follow Nonna's example from the Bible, 1 Corinthians 16:13,

Be on your guard, stand firm in the faith,
be courageous, be strong.
(*New American Bible,* emphasis added.)

Courage means believing in faith even when you are faced with the impossible, when you feel that, although you stand there with two outstretched arms wildly waving back and forth, God cannot see you. It takes courage to believe that a miracle may occur. And when that inexplicable event does occur, it takes courage to believe that it truly was the miracle you were praying for. It took courage for me to truly believe that God was not punishing me. It took courage to believe I was worthy in the eyes of God. It took courage for me to make it through what seemed the impossible. It is with God and through faith that I made it.

Three generations ago a miracle occurred in my family when the Blessed Virgin Mary and two angels appeared to my great-grandmother Giuseppina. A miracle so powerful, so pervasive its positive effect is felt one continent away and one hundred years later. From that Divine dispensation a presence of Divine protection and love was passed to Nonna. Nonna's unique understanding and reverent expression of the divine dispensation was her *Lezione Quattro*, Life Lesson Four: the courage to experience a benevolent and loving God. From Nonna's Life Lesson Four, I have felt God's prevailing compassion infuse hope into my weary or anxious soul. I have felt God's benevolence soothe my broken heart with the salve of knowing that my beloved departed are well and enveloped in a love that surpasses our understanding. I experienced the exhilarating energy of a miracle occurring. I now know the potency of prayer and the power of faith that enables miracles to happen...to me *and* to you.

May you possess the courage to:
- Believe in forgiveness and the healing balm that is derived from forgiving yourself and others.
- Believe your beloved departed are enveloped in a love so complete and warm it surpasses our understanding.
- Enter into a deeper relationship with God.
- Believe in the potency of prayer.
- Believe in the power of faith.
- Believe in the miracle that is occurring in you at this very moment.

Nonna and Lisa by the ever-present Blessed Mary statue in her
backyard. See story of Nonna's statue in Chapter 1.

Top right: Fr. Solanus Scapular given to me by Nonna.
See Fr. Solanus story in Chapter 10.

Epilogue

Learn more about Nonna's Life Lessons One through Seven and foster the Courage that lies within you and with which You Can!

Lezioni Uno-Tre (Lessons One –Three) *Coraggio! Lessons for Living from an Italian Grandmother Despite Illness, Pain and Loss* (copyright 2009)

Lezione Quattro (Lesson Four) *Coraggio! Lessons for Living from an Italian Grandmother: Courage to Believe in Miracles* (copyright **2010**)

Coraggio! Lessons for Living from an Italian Grandmother: Courage to Conquer Pain

Lezione Cinque (Lesson Five): The courage to discover new perspectives and approaches to dealing with physical and emotional pain. **(copyright** 2011)

Coraggio! Lessons for Living from an Italian Grandmother: The Courage to Grieve and to Honor (bring peace, love and joy to) *the End of Life*

Lezioni Sei & Sette (Lessons Six & Seven): Courage to honor the end-of-life and live each day as if you are creating your legacy. **(copyright** 2011)

www.WithCourageICan.com

My father, Pasquale, after lifting me from my wheelchair
and into his car,
and then storing the wheelchair in the car's trunk.
See story Chapter 5.

Bibliography

Chin, Thomas K, MD, *Rheumatic Heart Disease*, May 18, 2006, http://www.emedicine.com/ped/topic2007.htm.

Deuteronomy 5:6-21, Exodus 20:2-17, *Ten Commandments*, New International Version.

Father Solanus Guild, <http://www.solanuscasey.org>.

Fourteenth Dalai Lama, His Holiness Tenzin Gyatso, <u>Kindness, Clarity, and Insight</u>, Snow Lion Publications, 1984, p. 11.

Gallagher, Fr. Timothy M. OMV, *An Ignatian Introduction to Prayer: Spiritual Reflections According to the Spiritual Exercises*, Cross Road Publishing Co., 2008.

Gallagher, Fr. Timothy M., OMV, The Discernment of Spirits: An Ignatian Guide for Everyday Living, Cross Road Publishing Co., 2005.

Gumpert, Martin, *The Menace of Rheumatic Fever*, Abstract, *The Nation*, March 9, 1946.

Koenig, Harold G., M.D. & Lawson, Douglas M. Ph.D., *Faith in the Future: Healthcare, Aging, and the Role of Religion*, Templeton Foundation Press, 2004, pp. 77-97.

Koenig, Harold G., M.D., *The Healing Power of Faith: Science Explores Medicine's Last Great Frontier*, Simon & Schuster, 1999, pp. 233-240.

Kolodijchuk, Brian, M.C., Editor, *Mother Teresa, Come be my Light: The Private Writings of the "Saint of Calcutta,"* Doubleday, 2007, pp 210-217.

Le Chiese, SS. Pietro e Paolo, http://www.comunedipedivigliano.it.

Madonna Della Quercia, http://www.madonnadellaquercia.it/

Matthew 5:1-12, New International Version.

McCartney, Paul, & Lennon, John, *Let It Be*, released by The Beatles 1970.

Mercy Foundation, Solanus Casey: *Priest-Porter-Prophet*, Video, 2002.

Mother Teresa of Calcutta, *A Gift for God: Prayers and Meditations*, Harper & Row, 1975, pp. pp. 71, 72, 75.

Mother Teresa: The Early Years, <http://www.ewtn.com/motherteresa/life.htm>.

Psalms, Chapter 23, *The Psalm of David*, New American Bible.

Saint Therese of Liseux, Manuscrits autographiques, C 25r.

Solanus Casey Center, A Franciscan Ministry, http://www.solanuscenter.org.

Title page and above photos

Processioni per la Festa Della Madonna Della Quercia
(Procession for the Feast of the Madonna of the Oak)

In the 1500s the Madonna (Blessed Virgin Mary) appeared at the Oak Tree in the Visora forest of Calabria, Italy. That day and in the years that followed miraculous events occurred to the townsfolk who prayed at that site. Almost five hundred years later, on the last Sunday of August each year, hundreds of people gather to celebrate the Feast of the Madonna of the Oak in Conflenti, the neighboring town of my Nonno (grandfather) Francesco Gigliotti, Motto Santa Lucia, Provencia Catanzaro, Italy. The photographs were sent to Nonno and Nonna by Zio (Uncle) Ciccio Gigliotti (See below.)

My Nagymama Anna (right) and my mother holding my toddler hands (brother Peter to side). A couple years later Nagymama would hold my hand again as we walked down the Holy Cross Church aisle.
See story in Chapter 4.

Front cover photo: My mother Julia Barczay Gigliotti in her pre-teen years.

Back cover photos:
My mother holding newborn daughter Lisa in 1961;
photo taken by my father at the outset of his photographer, and television director and producer careers.
Nonna and Lisa beside Nonna's Madonna statue in her backyard; summer 1994.
Nonna in her First Holy Communion veil.